I0046472

Better Policy | Better Performance

.

Better Policy | Better Performance

*The Who, Why, and What
of Organizational Policy*

Rose Landry and donalee Moulton

BEP

BUSINESS EXPERT PRESS

Leader in applied, concise business books

Better Policy | Better Performance:
The Who, Why, and What of Organizational Policy

Copyright © Business Expert Press, LLC, 2025.

Cover design by Charlene Kronstedt

Interior design by S4Carlisle Publishing Services, Chennai, India

All rights reserved. No part of this publication may be reproduced, stored in a retrieval system, or transmitted in any form or by any means—electronic, mechanical, photocopy, recording, or any other except for brief quotations, not to exceed 400 words, without the prior permission of the publisher.

First published in 2025 by
Business Expert Press, LLC
222 East 46th Street, New York, NY 10017
www.businessexpertpress.com

ISBN-13: 978-1-63742-842-9 (paperback)
ISBN-13: 978-1-63742-843-6 (e-book)

Business Expert Press Strategic Management

First edition: 2025

10 9 8 7 6 5 4 3 2 1

EU SAFETY REPRESENTATIVE
Mare Nostrum Group B.V.
Mauritskade 21D
1091 GC Amsterdam
The Netherlands
gpsr@mare-nostrum.co.uk

Dedications

To my mother—just because :).
—Rose Landry

To Lisa. Faux daughter, who shares my love of policy—and my heart.
—donalee Moulton

Acknowledgments

There are many people to thank. We may have written this book, but the foundation was forged when we were in school learning concepts, techniques, and theories that would help to shape our understanding of policy in the years ahead. The foundation goes beyond knowledge, however. There are numerous people who took the time to explore issues with us, challenge us, and mentor us. We are in your debt.

We must also acknowledge the role family has played, patiently and supportively as we took time, slurped coffee, and Zoomed endlessly to draft chapters, debate ideas, and meet deadlines. We know the significant contribution you have made.

We would like to single out two people in particular deserving of our thanks. Gerry Martin, former director of the Saint Mary's University Executive and Professional Development program, embraced the concept of a policy certificate program for people in the field working with policy, enmeshed in policy, and moving into the policy realm. She was patient as the certificate program evolved, grew, and reached across North America and beyond.

Our deepest appreciation is also extended to Cheryl Enman, who read, reread, proofread, and then read this book again. She formatted it and reformatted it. And she never complained. For which we are immensely grateful.

Finally, our heartfelt thanks to the many students and clients we have had the privilege to work with over the years and who have taught us how policy lives and breathes in the real world.

Testimonials

"A must-read for leaders and decision makers who want to run efficient and successful organizations, Better Policy | Better Performance: The Who, Why, and What of Organizational Policy *by Rose Landry and donalee Moulton explains what policy is and the need for policies. It is also very practical. Starting with the critical question 'What do we need to achieve?' readers are offered a step-by-step guide to designing and implementing policies. Using real-world examples from iconic companies like Johnson & Johnson and Apple Inc., complemented by useful diagrams and charts, actional insights are provided. The book also includes important details on how to evaluate the effectiveness of policies.* Better Policy | Better Performance *is an essential guide for every business and organization."* —**Barbara Cottrell, President, Meta Research and Communications**

"Ms. Landry and Ms. Moulton, both with extensive experience in the field of policy, present a persuasive argument that effective organizational policy requires a holistic approach. Written in accessible language and supported by practical examples, this book will be a valuable resource whether you are responsible for policy development, implementation, or monitoring."—**Sharon Reashore, LL.B.**

"Throughout my career I have seen various approaches to developing and implementing policy and have come to the conclusion that good, even great, policy is about leadership at all levels in an organization, from the frontline to the Board. Understanding why a policy is needed, what its intent is, having a real opportunity for input on its development and participation in its ongoing evaluation are critical to the success of any policy. This book provides practical advice and helpful examples useful to understanding how great policies are developed and how they should evolve over time. If you are actively involved in policy work or wish to better understand policy, check this book out! I would have had this book dog eared from use had it been available to me during my career progression."—**Krista Connell, President, Fertiloam Inc.**

Keywords

policy; policy development; writing policy; organizational policy; public policy; procedures; decision making; performance; strategy; policy implementation; equity; evaluation; strategic planning

Contents

List of Figures

Introduction

This is a book about policy—the reality of policy and the promise.

The focus is on organizational policy. For many, this type of policy is contained in a policy document that describes what to do in a specific situation. Then there is another policy document that describes what to do in another specific situation. Many policies do that. But policy at its best goes beyond a distinct set of documents dealing with specific situations and compiled into a binder, digital or otherwise.

Policy at its most effective infuses an organization. It is driven by mission and vision; it appears in and is driven by strategic plans—even if they aren't labeled "policy." Policy is an inherent part of what an organization does and how it does it. It is more than a binder labeled "Policy." Policy is informed and reflected at all levels of the organization.

We have been working in the policy field for many decades, and we know many organizations do not yet see the promise in policy. They conceptualize policy as a layer, not as an integral component of their values, goals, and strategic actions. They operate at a more micro level, where policy dictates who, what, where, when, and, sometimes, why. This is a good place to start, but policy can and should be so much more. Savvy organizations know this.

In this book, we'd like to share with you what such organizations know, what they have told us over the past 35 years in classrooms, policy shops, strategic planning sessions, and policy reviews. Some of what we have to share will be old hat; some will be new. Some will make instant sense; some will be uncomfortable. From this vantage point, it is our hope that you can improve the way policy is developed and implemented in your organization.

This book is intended for all those who touch policy within their organizations: those who set policy; those who develop it; those who write it, communicate it, manage it, implement it, and review it—and even those who ignore it. While all aspects of policy rarely fall within the domain of one employee, understanding the overarching approach and the process is helpful no matter what your role.

Organizational policy is distinct from public policy. Public policy is broad, and it is fundamental to the state. It is a principle that guides action. In this regard, it is the foundation on which law is based, and it is ultimately about making and operationalizing decisions to drive corporate and individual citizen behaviors in ways that will (hopefully) enable and ensure their respective and shared rights and obligations like safety and privacy.

Organizational policy is about making and putting into practice decisions that will drive management and staff behaviors in ways that will (again hopefully) enable the organization to achieve and sustain success.

There is overlap, and there are critical distinctions between the two. Our focus is on policy inherent to an organization, and that includes government organizations. It does not include public policy, although it may be influenced and impacted by those polices.

In addition to discussing the context of policy and its importance to an organization, *Better Policy | Better Performance* explores practical issues related to development and implementation. We hope you find the tips and suggestions helpful. Ultimately, we hope you can take what you need from this book to make policy relevant and effective in your organization.

CHAPTER 1

Policy Thinking and Approach

It May Not Be What You Think It Is

This book is not a textbook. It's not a theoretical exploration of policy. It is not a discourse on public policy. It is not a magic template that will enable you to develop and implement policy in mere minutes.

So, now you know what you're not reading.

What you are reading is intended to be practical, useful, and informative. Our goal is to help shape your understanding of policy and how policy works—and can work—in your world. *Better Policy | Better Performance* is rooted in our combined experience as policy and communications analysts, practitioners, decision makers, teachers, and advisers. That experience is long and varied. It spans the public, private, and not-for-profit sectors; it spans industries from agriculture to zoology, from food service to pharmaceuticals. And it spans organizations of all shapes and sizes, from mom-and-pop shops to international organizations with thousands of employees.

We know how policy is understood and approached and how it shows up in different organizations, and we know what works well and what doesn't work so well. Topping the list of things we know: Policy means different things to different organizations.

Because policy is understood and approached differently by different organizations (sometimes even by different people within the same organization), it is important to begin by understanding what we mean when we refer to "policy" and to policy approaches. That understanding is the foundation on which this book is based.

What Is It?

Policy is one of those things that lots of people talk about (believe it or not) and everyone is subject to (also believe it or not). It seems to be everywhere and applied to everything, and yet it is surprisingly difficult to nail down exactly what "it" is.

When most of us think about policy, we think about "rules" and "policy statements." This is understandable. Rules are made, and they are communicated in policy statements on a regular basis. But policy statements are not the only source from which policy can be gleaned and rules are not the only things communicated in policy statements. So, it is safe to say that while policy may involve rules and policy statements are important, what policy is about is way more than that.

The truth is that there is no easy way to define policy because it is a multilayered term. It's kind of like an onion—when you start to peel away the layers, you'll find another layer underneath. And yes—you may cry.

What Does It Look Like?

High-level policy is the direction and course of action set by leadership—the organization's vision and mission and goals and the high-level strategies it puts in place to achieve them. These "policies" are often articulated in documents referred to as "strategic plans," but—make no mistake—they are in fact statements of policy.

At the Organizational Level

Policy enables and supports the design and establishment of a "system" (what the textbooks call organizational norms) using objectives, principles, values, parameters, and standards to guide and align the organization's focus, structure, functions, resources, and decisions in key areas. Ideally, this guidance and alignment will enable the strategy and the vision.

At a Process Level

Policy involves planning and developing, implementing, and managing that strategy and that system as it becomes reality and as it evolves.

There are three elements in this level:

- **Planning and development** are about informing and making decisions about the direction, strategy, and courses of action. It involves designing the "system" to enable the strategy—in other words, deciding what objectives, principles, values, approaches, and standards will be put in place to guide and align the organization's behaviors and decisions.
- **Implementing** that system, also called operationalizing it, includes putting in place the organizational infrastructure (structures, processes, and yes, even other policies) and communicating, inspiring, supporting, and/or compelling people to adopt the norms to enable it.
- **Managing policy**—here we monitor progress, measure impacts, and make adjustments as required to ensure the system and the strategy are operating as intended, that it is and will continue to be an effective means of achieving the organization's goals and realizing its vision.

At a Practical Level

As experienced by the people who interact in and with the organization, policy is quite simply what the organization does or does not do, what it accomplishes or doesn't accomplish, and what it values or doesn't value as reflected in its behavior and decisions.

This last level is particularly important. Regardless of what is intended or documented as "policy" and "strategy," actual policy and strategy are best reflected by what is actually happening. What an organization actually does or does not do will always reflect the policy and strategy that is truly in play, and that policy and strategy will lead to progress toward a direction and produce results. It will not, however, always reflect the intended strategy, make progress in the intended direction, or move you toward intended results. W. Edwards Deming, business theorist and economist, said it well, "Your system is perfectly designed to give you the results you are getting."

This multilayered view of policy does two things. First, it establishes the link between planning and policy. Second, it makes everything sound very strategic, orderly, deliberate, and well documented.

While the link between planning and policy is often recognized (witness the tendency of many large organizations to establish policy and planning shops), it is not always well understood. The implied order in the multilayered understanding of policy may or may not exist depending on how well the organization understands the link between policy and everything else.

Proving Policy Exists

Typically, when people ask if there is a policy, they are really asking whether a policy has been made explicit or formalized in documents like strategic plans and policy statements. But not all policies are explicit— some are implicit. Implicit policies are the ones that aren't written down but are reflected in the behaviors of the organization and its people.

Many professional organizations do not have written dress codes, for example, but try showing up for work as a bank teller in shorts and a tank top and see how long it takes for your boss to advise you that "this attire is not appropriate."

The reality is that most organizations have an "implicit" dress code policy and most people who work in them instinctively know what it is. This holds true even today when so many people work from home. It may not matter if you work in your pajamas if no one can see you, but attend an online meeting with cameras on, and chances are you're changing into a shirt or a sweater. The fact that we would not be comfortable wearing our pajama tops to meetings is evidence that a dress code policy exists.

There is good reason for not wearing our pajamas to work, of course. The goal is to inspire client/colleague confidence, and part of the strategy is to present an image of professionalism. This strategy is generally operationalized when staff and managers model, encourage, and enforce an existing norm of wearing or not wearing certain things to work in certain settings.

Implicit policy is a silent nod to the current state—it has the effect of directing or "allowing" staff and management to keep doing what they're doing (or not doing what they're not doing) because this behavior reflects the desired culture, focus, accountability, values, and more that the organization seeks to attain and exhibit.

On the positive side, that silent nod can be empowering. In essence, it says, "We trust your judgment." On the not-so-positive side, silence may signal false assumptions and/or indifference to things that may be important to customers, clients, and/or staff. For instance, it may reflect an erroneous assumption that customers always receive great service or that disrespectful behaviors never occur in the workplace.

Every staff member's behavior is organizational behavior. If leadership remains silent in the face of unprofessional or disrespectful behaviors, it is in effect saying that changing them is not important or a priority. The policy is to focus on other things.

Left unattended, these sorts of behaviors can erode staff and client/customer confidence and render the organization a less attractive place to work or shop or eat or.... Put differently, if it matters to staff, customers, clients, patients, shareholders, and others in the work environment, digital or physical, it should matter to leadership.

Bottom Line

From a policy perspective, what an organization doesn't do can be just as important as what it does.

Policy Authority and Style

An organization exists anywhere more than one person comes together to do something. A family, a group of friends, a government, a company, or an association—all can be considered an organization.

Policy is set or approved by the most senior authority in any organization.

The most senior authority could be a group (e.g., management teams, executives, boards, cabinets) or a person (e.g., mom, CEO, deputy minister).

Friends, for instance, want to explore their boundaries without fear of getting in trouble at home, so they adhere to a code—perhaps "What happens in Vegas stays in Vegas"; moms want their kids to develop healthy eating habits so they will routinely buy certain foods and rarely buy others; CEOs want to maximize profit, so there are certain markets, processes, or sales practices they will focus on, follow, or use; and governments have a duty to protect the public, so there are certain behaviors they will promote or penalize.

The key here is that when policies are made, they only apply to those people, to those issues, and in those settings over which the policy maker has authority. Moms, for example, set policy for their own kids—not their neighbors' kids. When the neighborhood kids are playing in her house, her policies will apply (e.g., they will eat the types of foods she provides) but when they go home, they will only eat the types of food approved of in their own home.

It is the same way for organizations. Boards and CEOs have authority over the whole organization, VPs over the functional areas within the organization that they are accountable for, and managers over their units.

All senior authorities have a style, and that style will have a significant impact on the organization's approach to policy.

In organizations where the most senior authority has a "macro" leadership/management style, the overarching process tends to work as a cascade of policy and authority.

The most senior authority sets the first level of policy. That first level defines the expectations for the organization, the overall strategy, and parameters for subsequent levels of policy, which, in turn, sets the expectations, strategy, and parameters for component parts and/or specific functions of the organization. In effect, beginning at the top, each layer of the organization delegates authority to the next layer, establishing a sort of sandbox within which the next layer has authority or flexibility to exercise discretion.

This "macro" approach enables flexibility and responsiveness. The goal is not to make sure everyone does or decides what the CEO would do or decide; it is to ensure that everyone's actions and decisions are aligned to move the organization in a particular direction and to enable the flexibility and agility required to respond to individual situations and to adapt to quickly changing circumstances.

Figure 1.1 below provides a view of the typical distribution of policy and policy related authority in a macro led organization. Figure 1.2 reflects the level scope for flexibility/responsiveness enabled by this macro approach. The arrow represents the goal or direction, its width represents the degree of discretion allowed, and each of the dots represents a decision at the program or operational level.

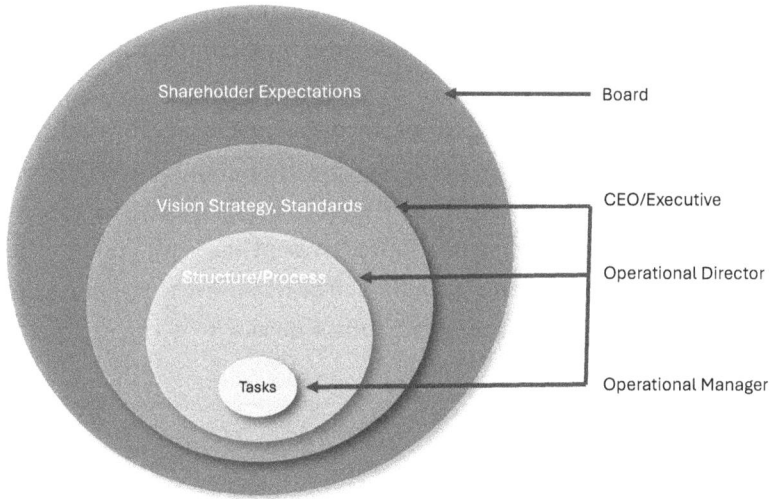

Figure 1.1 Macro Approach—Distribution of Authority

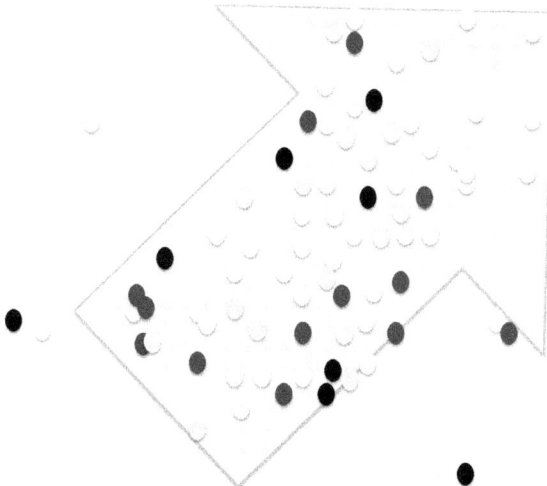

Figure 1.2 Macro Approach—Scope for Flexibility/Responsiveness

Approaching policy this way empowers people within the organization to make decisions at the process and task levels and enables leaders to hold people accountable for the exercise of discretion and the results of the decisions they make—and not simply for doing what they're told to do. The risk is that those decisions will sometimes be disconnected from the strategy and/or have unintended and/or unwanted implications. This is not always a bad thing—trying new ways of doing things can lead to innovative ways of achieving better results. On the other hand, depending on the frequency or magnitude of negative implications, it can become problematic.

In more micro-led/managed organizations where decisions are more centralized, CEO/executive policy statements tend to focus on and include things like process and tasks (Figure 1.3). This effectively narrows the ability to apply discretion at lower levels of the organization; it restricts the flexibility of the organization to be responsive to realities on the floor and individual situations or to adapt quickly to changing circumstances (Figure 1.4).

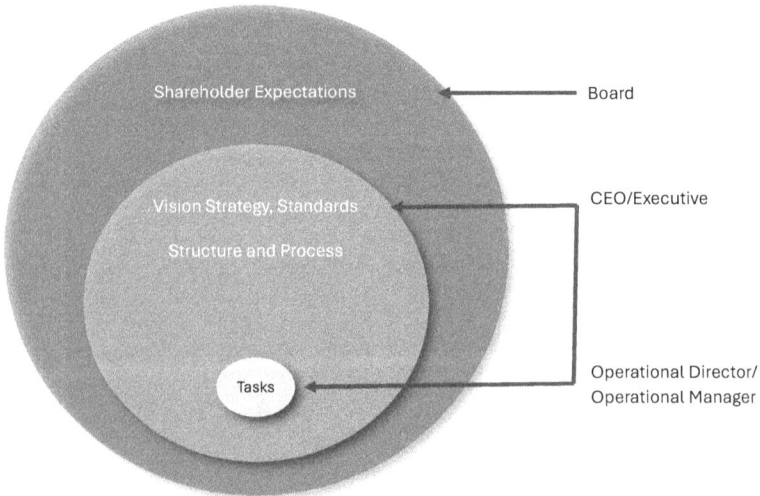

Figure 1.3 Micro Approach—Delegation of Authority

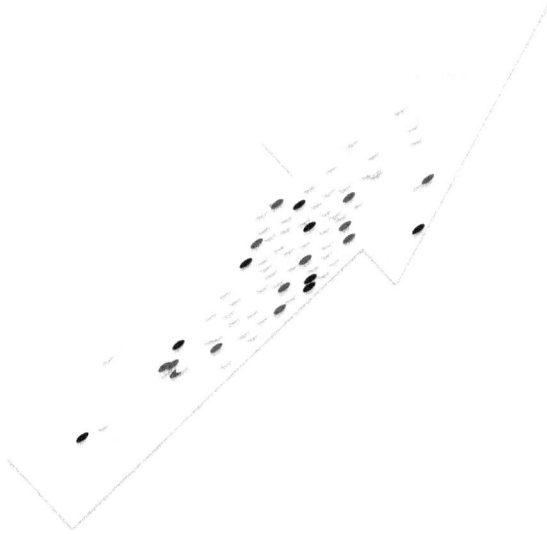

Figure 1.4 Micro Approach—Scope for Flexibility/Responsiveness

Accountability in these organizations tends to focus on the notion of compliance and whether people are doing what they have been told or asked to do. Accountability for results rests solely with the CEO/ executive.

There are good reasons why different types of organizations may lean toward one or another of these approaches. Military, police, and health providers tend more toward micro policy approaches. Their risk tolerance is low for good reason—lives are at stake—and it is critical that processes and steps are predictable and standardized. Consulting organizations, on the other hand, require a high level of flexibility to stay ahead of management/leadership trends and to be responsive to multiple clients whose needs and circumstances might be very different. They tend toward a more macro approach to enable that flexibility.

The thing to remember is that style matters. It will shape the nature of accountability in your organization, the level of standardization/predictability, the degree of responsiveness, and the speed with which your organization is able to adapt to changing circumstances.

Policy Scope and Approach

Anywhere there is a vision, goals, a strategy, and an action being taken to operationalize that strategy, there is policy.

Few policies, if any, stand alone. Most are but one component in a larger network of policies that together reflect an organization's course of action or strategy to achieve its goals and visions. Individual policy statements typically focus on the action part of the equation and rarely reflect the fullness of a strategy.

For example, a well-designed, fully implemented, and operational workplace health and safety strategy will function to reduce or eliminate the risk and impact of workplace-related injury and illness on individuals (health and wellness) and the organization (productivity and performance). That strategy will be articulated as a network of policies that address any number of separate physical and/or emotional risk areas such as:

- Fitness for work
- Ergonomics
- Safety equipment
- Machine use
- Hazardous substance handling and storage
- Respect in the workplace.

Those policies, in turn, will inform the purchase of tools and equipment; the establishment of structures, processes, and behaviors; and the definition or redefinition of performance. Once in place, performance management mechanisms enable the reduction or elimination of work-related health and safety risks.

That's the dream: a clear policy objective, a plausible strategy, the development and operationalization of a network of well-aligned, well-articulated, enabling policies.

The reality is that many organizational policies do not begin with a vision or higher-level goal in mind. Nor are they developed as component pieces of broader strategies. Rather, many policies are developed to address micro issues in the moment and as they emerge.

Let's explore this a bit more.

Strategic Versus Incremental

Some organizations develop a fully comprehensive policy that is intentionally designed to address and connect all levels of policy as described in our earlier definition. This starts with an overarching vision, goals, and strategy.

Johnson & Johnson is one of those organizations. The multinational pharmaceutical, biotechnology, and medical technologies megacorporation has been in business for over 130 years and is consistently ranked as one of Fortune 500's most successful and admired companies. Its policies are rooted in what it calls *Our Credo*. This clearly describes its overall vision, values, goals, and high-level strategy:

> We believe our first responsibility is to the patients, doctors and nurses, to mothers and fathers and all others who use our products and services. In meeting their needs, everything we do must be of high quality. We must constantly strive to provide value, reduce our costs and maintain reasonable prices. Customers' orders must be serviced promptly and accurately. Our business partners must have an opportunity to make a fair profit.
>
> We are responsible to our employees who work with us throughout the world. We must provide an inclusive work environment where each person must be considered as an individual. We must respect their diversity and dignity and recognize their merit. They must have a sense of security, fulfillment and purpose in their jobs.
>
> Compensation must be fair and adequate and working conditions clean, orderly and safe. We must support the health and well-being of our employees and help them fulfill their family and other personal responsibilities. Employees must feel free to make suggestions and complaints. There must be equal opportunity for employment, development and advancement for those qualified. We must provide highly capable leaders, and their actions must be just and ethical.
>
> We are responsible to the communities in which we live and work and to the world community as well. We must help people be healthier by supporting better access and care in more places around the world. We must be good citizens—support good works and charities, better health and education, and bear our fair share of taxes. We must

maintain in good order the property we are privileged to use, protecting the environment and natural resources.

Our final responsibility is to our stockholders. Business must make a sound profit. We must experiment with new ideas. Research must be carried on, innovative programs developed, investments made for the future and mistakes paid for. New equipment must be purchased, new facilities provided and new products launched. Reserves must be created to provide for adverse times.

When we operate according to these principles, the stockholders should realize a fair return.

The vision, values, goals, and strategy highlighted in Johnson & Johnson's *Our Credo* are further defined in separate published policy statements, each focused on a specific key topic area such as corporate governance, diversity, equity and inclusion, employee development, and total health and well-being. Each policy statement articulates the company's understanding of and commitment to its vision, goals, and strategy for the topic area and names the principles, values, parameters, approaches, and rules that will guide its decisions and behaviors as well as the structures that will be established to enable them.

Johnson & Johnson understands and approaches policy the way we described it earlier. Their approach is deliberate and comprehensive. It is a strategic, visionary approach. In the *Harvard Business Review* article "How Johnson & Johnson Made Hard Decisions During COVID," Joanne Waldstreicher describes how that approach gets operationalized.

A policy decision was required to deal with an ethical issue. An antiviral medication to treat HIV patients was being used off book by frontline doctors who thought it may be an effective way to treat COVID-19. Demand was growing. Johnson & Johnson did not have sufficient supply to meet both sets of needs, and, despite what the doctors believed, the company was not convinced that this particular antiviral medication would be effective for COVID-19 patients.

The company went back to its credo and:

- Grounded itself in its responsibilities
- Developed a framework to guide decisions about using medications approved for other uses as possible COVID-19 treatments

- Considered the science
- Assessed its capacity to meet the demand related to both HIV and COVID-19
- Decided not to divert the drugs from HIV patients to COVID-19 patients.

This example reflects a strategic and integrated approach to policy. It took time and required that the company resist the urge so many companies feel to act now.

Many of you will say this integrated, reasoned, and comprehensive approach is not what happens where you work. You are very likely right.

In our experience, many organizations take what they likely feel is a faster approach to policy. Faster or not, they take a hugely different approach. They start with individual topics, or even subtopics, and publish policy statements that skip vision, goals, and strategy and move directly to process, roles, responsibilities, and rules. The link to a higher-level vision and strategy is unclear, if it exists at all.

These organizations understand and approach policy quite differently than the way we do. Their policies tend to be developed to address individual situations as they arise and reflect an incremental, and sometimes fragmented, understanding of and approach to planning and policy development. The overall intended vision and strategy are not generally designed; instead, they emerge over time in linkages that appear as more and more individual situations get addressed. The linkages may or may not be deliberate, and often, even when they exist, they are not comprehensive enough to avoid disconnection in the direction being given to staff and by extension in the link between what is happening on the ground, the results that will inevitably be produced, and the results the organization wants.

For example, many organizations we have worked with over the years have had visions that involve customer or client service excellence. They highlight adaptability and flexibility as key characteristics of an excellent service culture and identify employee empowerment as a key component of the strategy to operationalize that flexibility and adaptability. Many of those same organizations have customer service (and other) policies that focus heavily on standardizing service processes and responses. Standardization is about establishing consistency or, in customer service terms, about ensuring that every customer is treated the "same" way.

Consistency can be a good thing. It doesn't just create order; for example, it communicates to customers that, if you like a refreshing Coca-Cola in Baltimore, you will be just as refreshed in Montreal and Beijing because the Coke you purchase in one place will taste the same in all the others.

However, this emphasis on consistency can also inhibit flexibility. Some standardization policies don't leave room for discretion, so the focus on "sameness" is what ends up being operationalized. Without room for discretion, employees cannot be responsive to individual customer needs in any but the most predictable set of circumstances. The conversation at the desk or on the phone is always the same:

"Would it be possible to…?"
"I'm sorry, but our policy doesn't allow for that."
"But couldn't you make an exception?"
"I'm sorry, but there are no exceptions."

Such situations often end with a frustrated customer and an employee who is relieved the conversation is over.

The disconnect is clear. The strategy to operationalize flexible, adaptable service is not in play. The company's actual strategy is to operationalize consistency or sameness of service, and the result will sometimes be that fewer customers may be or remain loyal over time.

This disconnect is not the fault of the employee. If the focus of policies is absolute consistency, staff are simply doing what they have been directed to do.

Bottom Line

Regardless of an organization's definition and approach, all organizations have written and unwritten policies, and those policies will influence the organization's focus, culture, governance, management, and results.

One Last Thing

Despite the general tendency to distinguish between public policy and organizational policy, from a practical perspective, the steps in the development process and onward is much the same. The exception is in the scope and complexity of the authorities, the issues, the interest holders.

Governments have a wide range of options with respect to how they will encourage, enable, and motivate people within their jurisdictions to adopt the cultural and behavioral norms they are advocating. If and/or when that doesn't work, they can use legislation and regulation to compel adoption and compliance regardless of individual citizen's preferences.

These levers are not typically available to organizations; they cannot "compel" adoption or compliance in the same way. It is true that organizations have levers that are used to promote or compel compliance—for example, rewards, discipline, or dismissal. However, as employees you can always choose to leave the organization if you don't agree with its policies. Leaving your state, province, or country because you disagree with public policy, however, is a much more difficult decision. Organizational leaders know this and so inherently understand that policies will guide rather than compel behaviors and that they will require a higher level of buy-in to enable adoption.

We'll leave the last word on policy to Ronald Reagan, former U.S. President, who said, "Surround yourself with the best people you can find, delegate authority, and don't interfere as long as the policy you've decided upon is being carried out."

CHAPTER 2

Setting the Policy Agenda and Developing Policy

Kinda Like Creating World Peace

Policy is not—and should not be—random. There is an accepted and effective set of interconnected core processes that guide policy creation and realization from concept to completion.

The core processes work together to enable organizations to:

Set the policy agenda. This is the starting point. It's focused on deciding what issues, challenges, or opportunities require attention, specifically a change in organizational strategy and/or behavior.

Develop the policy. This is the foundation of the policy. Here data are gathered, research is conducted, and information is analyzed to inform and make decisions about what the goal, the course of action, and future organizational behaviors will be.

Implement the policy. This is much more than sending an e-mail with a policy document attached. It requires designing and putting in place the infrastructure (communication, structures, processes, training, and more) to enable and support (operationalize) the new strategy/behavior.

Monitor and evaluate the policy. This is the ongoing management piece. Here data are gathered and analyzed to understand if the necessary infrastructure is in place, if the desired behaviors are occurring, and if the targets and goals are being achieved.

Each process includes several steps that are critical to the overall success of a policy. The interrelationship between them is often described as cyclical—as a policy cycle. The sequencing of those processes is not as linear as the notion of a "cycle" implies though. In fact, there is significant overlap. For example:

- Agenda setting *should* be informed by the policy development, implementation, and evaluation processes. This enables issues to be more fully understood, scoped, and uncovered.
- Policy development *should* begin with clear measurable goals (e.g., to maintain, increase, or decrease something) and targets. These, in turn, inform the evaluation framework and the data collection and reporting infrastructure that should be in place through the implementation process to enable the organization to monitor, manage, and evaluate progress and performance.
- Policy implementation strategies and the associated requirements, costs, and timelines *should* be well understood by the end of the policy formulation process so that decision makers can understand whether a policy option can be implemented at all and, if so, within what timeframe and budget.

We say "should" because in our experience the processes aren't always or even generally undertaken in this integrated way.

Some organizations, for example, wait until long after the policy is implemented to articulate its specific measurable goals or think about what data they ought to have been collecting and monitoring to manage or evaluate the policy. As a result,

- Many evaluations start back at the beginning with a need to get clarity about what the original goals were.
- Many evaluation reports begin with a finding that the data required to inform the evaluation are unavailable or incomplete. These reports usually end with a recommendation to put in place mechanisms to begin collecting that data.

Other organizations skip the steps within the development and implementation processes altogether. They assume that communication is all that is required to implement a policy and that, once the policy users have read, heard, and understood what's required of them, they will simply do it.

This approach rarely works. Indeed, it rarely goes smoothly and almost always results in a need to circle back and address the planning, implementation, and execution component that was skipped.

How do we know this? It's in plain view. All you have to do is look at the policy statements in your organization's policy manuals and find the ones that are languishing—like all of those lofty and comprehensive diversity visions and policy statements put in place prior to the 2020s. Many of these simply sat as idle aspirations until COVID-19 and the Black Lives Matter movement heightened awareness of the need to "do something." Many of those policies still sit as idle aspirations today.

To know that skipping functions or steps in their processes doesn't go smoothly, all you have to do is to think about all of those policies that took exponentially longer to be impactful than organizations thought they would.

Many organizations introduced no-smoking policies in the 1990s. The objective was to eliminate the smell, debris, and health hazards associated with smoking from the work environment. The goal was to achieve and maintain a smoke-free workplace.

In many cases, the strategy to achieve that goal was simply to ban or limit where people could smoke, but, other than communicating this ban, not much else was done to enable the policy to succeed—to have smokers embrace the policy at the highest level or accept it at the barest minimum. Many organizations went through several rounds before landing on an effective policy and implementation strategy. As some will remember, it looked something like this:

- Round 1
  - **Policy goal**. To achieve and maintain a smoke-free workplace.
  - **Policy strategy**. A ban on smoking anywhere inside but the lunchroom.
  - **Implementation strategy**. Write and publish a policy statement to communicate there will be no smoking at desks, only in the lunchroom.
  - **What people did**. Went to the lunchroom to smoke. Some brought their work there and set up shop.

- ○ **The impact**. All smoking was concentrated in a single area that was hard to get near without your eyes watering, and the smoke drifted out from this space to fill the workplace. Complaints about smoking in the workplace continued.
- Round 2
  - ○ **Policy goal**. No change.
  - ○ **New policy strategy**. A ban on smoking inside the building.
  - ○ **Implementation strategy**. Produce a new policy statement to communicate the new policy: no smoking in the building—only outside.
  - ○ **What people did**. Went outside to smoke—usually right beside the entrance and often without an ash can.
  - ○ **The impact**. The "office" was smoke-free and the entryways became littered with butts and smelled like an ashtray. People coming into the building (staff and clients alike) had to pass through a wall of smoke to enter. Complaints about smoking continued and complaints about the mess created began.
- Round 3—Let's try this again.
  - ○ **Policy goal**. No change.
  - ○ **New policy strategy**. A ban on smoking anywhere within X feet of the building.
  - ○ **Implementation strategy**. Produce a new policy statement to communicate no smoking within X feet of the building.
  - ○ **What people did**. Went X feet away to smoke where there was no shelter and still no ash cans. Took longer breaks to allow for "travel time."
  - ○ **Impact**. Finally, a workplace free from smoke—and an unsightly pile of butts on the property and lost productivity. Complaints about the mess continued, complaints about smokers taking longer breaks began, and smokers started to complain about being out in the rain.
- Round 4—Now we've got it.
  - ○ **Policy goal**. No change.
  - ○ **Policy strategy**. No change.

- ○ **New implementation strategy:**
  - ▪ Continue to communicate there is no smoking within X feet of the building.
  - ▪ Put in place infrastructure and processes to enable this:
    - • Set up shelters from rain, and so on.
    - • Place ash cans in and near the shelters.
    - • Put signs up in the shelters reminding people to use the ash cans.
    - • Establish a grace period after which performance management vis-à-vis extended breaks would be initiated.
- ○ **What people did.** Quit smoking, reduced the number of cigarettes they smoked, and/or went X feet away to smoke, used the shelters and ash cans, and returned to their desks at the appropriate time.
- ○ **The impact.** A smoke-free workplace, tidy grounds, restored productivity.

The optimists among you may say that these four rounds actually reflect a phased implementation or change management strategy that was designed to ease people into a new norm. That would be true if it had been planned this way from the beginning, although it is hard to imagine any organization planning to make its entryways inhospitable as a way of easing staff into anything. The organizations we have worked in and with, though, either weren't committed to the policy (were smokers and didn't want to stop smoking at their desks) or just didn't think it through—they skipped implementation planning.

When the policy development and implementation processes are abridged this way, it is generally because leaders feel pressure to act quickly, or not enough time and resources are given to move through the processes and their steps effectively. In the end, little or no time or resources are saved because of the need to circle back and fill in the gaps.

Bottom Line

It's important to consider each of the policy processes, recognize their interconnectedness, and undertake them in a way that enables you to manage their dependencies.

Setting the Agenda

Agenda setting is first and foremost about determining what challenges and opportunities are "policy issues." How do you know if something is a policy issue? Ask yourself this: Is change needed to address a concern? Is there an opportunity we need to better access? Is there a behavior (that is counterproductive to our goals or strategy) we'd like to change? These are all questions linked to policy. Answering them is a starting point. The agenda-setting process is generally the least formal of the policy processes because it is happening all the time—sometimes as part of a formal agenda-setting exercise and sometimes over coffee in the lunchroom or during a game of golf.

Challenges and opportunities don't generally just appear. They emerge over time and are often connected to things that are happening in the world in which your organization operates. Those "things" are reflected in major trends and events in the broader environment such as:

- The COVID-19 pandemic
- Widespread and increasing public demand for "green" workplaces and products
- The introduction of "disruptive" technology and artificial intelligence (AI).

"Those things" are also reflected in localized trends and events such as:

- Significant changes in government or organizational leadership
- Customer and employee complaints or requests
- Competitors gaining traction.

The trends and events present issues (challenges and opportunities) you may want to address in policy.

Major issues eventually land on everyone's agenda. More localized issues may or may not, depending on where they exist. Whatever the case, whether and when they land, is a function of the organization's awareness of the issue and its perception about whether or not it matters.

Awareness. Organizations typically become aware of issues through one or more of several sources, including the following:

- Close external sources like clients, constituents, and customers
- Other external sources like media, industry associations, professional publications, vendors, and lobbyists
- Personal sources like family, friends, and neighbors (never underestimate the power of familiarity)
- Internal sources like staff and management.

The more sources that identify and publicize an issue, the more likely it is to capture the attention of organizational leaders.

Perception. Once aware of an issue, leaders need to decide whether it is significant enough to require action. That decision will depend on how likely they believe it is that the opportunity or risk will materialize and the magnitude of impact they think it will have on the organizational goals.

Figure 2.1 offers a simple view of how this kind of thinking would impact the decision about whether and when an issue should be placed on the policy agenda.

For most organizations, the greater the probability the trend will be impactful and the higher the impact could be, the more important it is to address it—as a priority agenda item.

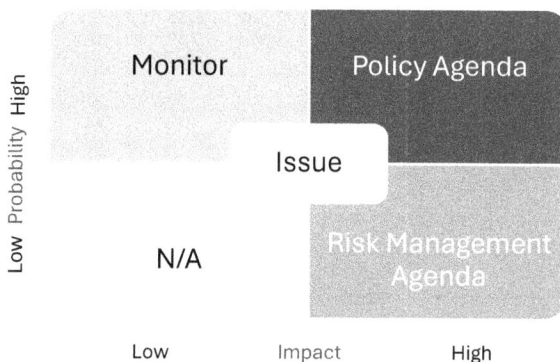

Figure 2.1 Prioritizing Policy Issues

An organization's culture and its approach to planning policy will determine if and where an issue will end up in the quadrants in Figure 2.1.

Culture is reflected in many organizational characteristics and manifests in all core policy processes as a whole and in agenda setting in particular. Two factors are critical: the organization's policy focus and its policy lens.

Policy Focus

Policy focus refers to the degree to which an organization concentrates on what is happening now versus what may and/or will happen in the future. This focus will determine whether the organization's culture/approach will tend to be more reactive or proactive.

Most organizations make it their business to at least stay informed about what is happening. But some stop here; their policy agendas tend to be challenge driven or reactive and focused on operational-level issues.

Other organizations are more proactive. They monitor and project trends to do one or both of the following two things:

- Anticipate what will happen in the future—these agendas may be either challenge or opportunity driven and tend to focus on longer-term, higher-level issues.
- Anticipate and then influence or drive the trends themselves—these agendas tend to be futuristic and high level.

Apple Inc., for example, built its reputation by anticipating what people would want or need in the future. Apple's cofounder Steve Jobs once said, "By the time you build something based on customer requests, they'll want something new." His strategy was to focus on anticipating consumer needs and wants and on creating products that would define and meet their future expectations.

To enable that focus and make asking that question intuitive, Jobs needed to establish a culture and system of creativity and innovation. When he returned to Apple in 1997 as CEO, he focused the policy agenda on aligning the organization with that culture and that strategy. It was essential to establish policies and put in place structures and processes that would guide, enable, and foster an innovative culture and a futuristic product design system.

In their 2020 article, "How Apple Is Organized for Innovation," Joel M. Podolny and Morten T. Hansen describe how Apple's structures and processes are aligned to enable an innovative culture, practices, and behaviors. This culture and focus gave rise to an ongoing futuristic agenda that enabled the development and introduction of innovative products that have changed the way we interact not only with technology but also with each other. For example, the iPhone was introduced in 2007. It provided consumers with a simple-to-use touchscreen on a handheld device with the functionality of a phone, a camera, a music player, and a computer all in one.

The iPhone drove Apple's global success and forced other companies to make change a priority on their policy agendas—to shift their focus to compete with Apple. Some companies recognized the opportunities and risks early and were quick to act. Those companies (e.g., Samsung Electronics Co., Ltd., and Google LLC) have remained competitive.

Others, including Research in Motion (RIM), the reigning king of smartphones in 2007, either didn't understand or simply underestimated the need to change and didn't place it on the agenda until it was too late. As a result, the company's share price dropped from $137.41 in 2007 to $14.80 in 2011. As of the time of this writing, RIM, now doing business as BlackBerry Limited, had a share price of $3.07.

Policy Lens

It's called the policy lens, and it shapes how your organization understands and thinks about policy. And it impacts every element of the policy function beginning with agenda setting.

The scope of the policy lens shapes what questions you ask as an organization, what sources you rely on for information, and how you receive, process, and interpret information in general and on any given issue.

Have you ever been in a situation where you have felt differently about an experience or thought about a situation differently than some or all of the people around you? You all hear exactly the same words or go through exactly the same motions, but you hear or experience them very differently.

For example, imagine a woman in her mid-50s whose teenage son arrives home with a tattoo. He's excited and proud. He's found a way to express his individuality. He thinks it's beautiful, and he's thrilled. She thinks it's kind of beautiful too. She also thinks: you've scarred your body! People will think you've joined a gang, now you'll never get a job! And … how are you going to feel about that thing when you're 40?!

His sources of information: popular culture and his friends.

His agenda: finding and implementing ways to display his new tattoo, like buying and wearing short-sleeved shirts.

Her sources of information: her experience as a person living and working in settings where, until recently, tattoos were taboo.

Her agenda: finding ways to live with it, to understand and appreciate that the tattoo really was an expression of his individuality and would not lead to gang activities or poor job prospects.

They have different lenses, different interpretations of exactly the same thing, and as a result, they have different agendas. Organizations are the same.

When information about COVID-19 first began circulating in North America, most organizations (and people) barely registered the information provided. It was a whisper. Something was happening on the other side of the world, something about a few people catching some sort of flu. No big deal and nothing to do with us. No need to seek additional information. Just keep doing what you're doing.

Most of us had no experience with or professional expertise in public health crises. We didn't seek sources of information other than media, so our information was limited, and our timeframe was immediate—we were thinking about what was happening here and, in those initial moments, COVID-19 was not happening here. As a result, most of us and most of our organizations initially ignored COVID-19 or assumed there was no need to react. The issue landed in the bottom left-hand quadrant: low probability, low impact—no action. Therefore, this COVID-19 thing did not make it on to our policy agenda.

For some organizations, however, the issue landed plunk in the upper right-hand quadrant in Figure 2.1 (high probability/high impact—a high-priority agenda item) and became a key component of the policy agenda of organizations like the World Health Organization (WHO). Like Apple, the WHO is committed to tracking, anticipating, and influencing trends (in this case, health trends). They raised the alarm.

WHO was not alone—other health organizations, researchers, and practitioners who had dealt with SARS in 2003, for example, received and processed the information WHO shared (the same information the rest of us received) very differently from most of us. For them, that first media article was an alarm. It signaled the presence of a virus that could easily and quickly pass to and from humans and from which there was no protection. They heard evidence of a looming health crisis: a pandemic. For them, this initial information was a call to action. It landed on their agendas immediately.

The lens these organizations used was global and rooted in specialized knowledge and experience. They gathered and sought out more specialized information. They had a duty to inform and protect, and, therefore, their timeframe was predictive: What was going to happen?

For these organizations, what happened next was the initiation of the policy development function. They asked:

- What do we need to achieve?
- What do we need to do to achieve this?

Most other people and organizations (except those with specialized experience and knowledge) did not initially believe that COVID-19 would impact their lives or alter their priorities. As we became better-informed and as the threat moved closer to home, we paid more attention. But it was not until the crisis actually landed on our doorsteps and there was no choice (because governments took action and states of emergency were declared) that most people and organizations realized the threat to their priorities and began to set new courses of action.

Our lenses didn't change. What did change was the immediacy of the threat and our access to information. Information that made it clear this virus would impact our lives, our lifestyles, and our organizations if we didn't do things differently.

COVID-19 revolutionized the workplace and service industries. The iPhone revolutionized the smartphone industry and the way we interact with each other. Both drove revolutionary change. However, the nature of the issues they reflected and the scope, risk, and the pace at which these emerged were significantly different. From an agenda-setting perspective, that difference lay in the type and level of threat and the urgency the issue presented.

The iPhone phenomenon reflected an opportunity and a risk that organizations could choose to or not to choose to pursue. It took a few years to reach the tipping point at which virtually all mobile players felt compelled to make a shift—to actively set new directions in an effort to take a bite out of the Apple.

COVID-19, on the other hand, was a global health crisis whose threat quickly went from distant to immediate. The first cluster was identified in Wuhan, China, in December 2019. By February 2020, it had spread to 28 other countries, including Canada, the United States, and Mexico, and, by the end of March 2020, all three North American countries had declared national states of emergency and their provincial and state governments were introducing policies requiring multiple measures (e.g., masks, social distancing, workplace shutdowns) that made it difficult if not impossible for people and organizations to survive without making fundamental changes to the way they conducted their lives and businesses.

There came a tipping point when putting COVID-19 on personal and organizational policy agendas was not a choice—it was an imperative. For some, it was personal, a literal matter of life and death; for others, it was the "right" thing to do to protect other people; and, for still others, it was simply a matter of reacting to widespread changes in behavior that were impacting their organizational goals (for instance, shoppers were shifting to businesses with delivery options) and/or staying on the right side of the law.

In any event, once you or your organization determine there is a need to or are forced to make choices about what action to take, the issue goes live and is placed on the agenda for policy formulation/development.

Bottom Line

This is where the policy development process is triggered—when you or your organization determines there is a need to or is forced to make choices about what action to take.

Most events and changes in the environment are not as widely impactful as the depth and breadth of opportunity that came with the introduction of iPhone or the threat of COVID-19. Nor are they typically announced with the bang and exposure of the iPhone or states of emergency.

In fact, many of the changes that lead to high-level policy development evolve over time and can be anticipated by keeping track of public, business, government, and technology trends. In organizations that track those trends and anticipate their future implications, like Apple and the WHO, being on the agenda tends to trigger the policy development process at the highest level, thinking about what an issue means for key organizational directions and whether those directions must or should change. If shifts in direction are recommended, this will necessitate rethinking goals and strategies and redesigning other policies to align with new directions. In this case, the development process takes the form of strategic planning first and lower-level policy formulation/development next.

In other organizations where the focus is more on what's happening now or in the very near term, being on the agenda tends to trigger policy review/formulation processes at a lower (topic or subtopic) level. Most of our students and many of our clients are from organizations that trigger the development process at this level.

Policy Development

Once an issue is on the policy agenda, it triggers the policy development process. This is the process through which information is gathered and analyzed to inform policy decisions—decisions about what action will be taken if any.

Regardless whether the process is triggered at the highest or the lowest level of policy, the development process and the steps within it tend to look the same. Indeed, it has looked the same from a high-level perspective for decades. Figure 2.2 lays out the basic steps.

Simple, right? Yep. The process itself really is quite simple, and we all move through it in one form or another, with varying degrees of rigor, any time we make a decision—policy or otherwise.

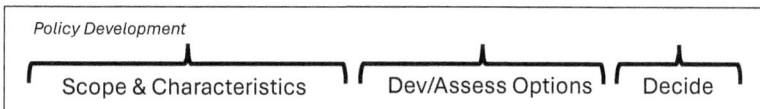

Figure 2.2 High Level Steps in the Policy Development Process

The level of effort that gets applied and the time and resources dedicated to it will vary depending on the person or the organization and their perception of the issue and what is a reasonable investment of time and effort to address it.

Some organizations do not spend enough time or resources on the development process. Leaders may feel pressure to "act" now either because they waited too long to put the issue on the policy agenda and time is running out (as may have been the case with RIM in the earlier example) or because they assume that they already know what the issue is and what the policy should be so they simply direct the policy staff to "write" a policy that reflects those assumptions.

The result is the sort of "try and try again" policy development process reflected in the "No Smoking" example. The ensuing policies may or may not address the root issues, and even if they do, they do not typically address them fully enough to avoid having to repeat the process again and again. We worked with one large organization that had over 20 separate smoking-related policies, some providing completely different directions to staff.

There are some situations that force an incremental approach. COVID-19, for example, created a situation where organizations were forced to make major "policy" decisions within days or weeks. The intention though was not to develop policy but to put interim measures in place. In fact, in the early days the term "COVID measures" was used much more often than "COVID policies." Had the pandemic been over after a few weeks, many organizations would have reversed these "measures" and returned to business as usual. It wasn't over in a few weeks though. The lockdowns and restrictions that led to things like remote work and virtual service delivery were in place off and on over the course of 2 years, and, by the time they ended, they had effectively changed the culture of work in many if not most industries—and they took on the force of policy.

Now, in the shadow of the pandemic, many organizations are seeing the need to circle back to those "policies" and initiate fuller, more deliberate development processes. They would do well to start by thinking through the scope of the issues they are dealing with and to define clear parameters to guide their development and decision making.

Scope and Parameters

Scoping helps to center and plan the rest of the development process. It involves starting with the "issue" that has been identified and figuring out:

- Who should be involved?
- What is the starting point?
- What else is happening?
- What is the real or "root" issue?
- What is the goal?
- Is there a need to change high-level (policy strategy) or use lower-level policy?
- What criteria will be applied to identify feasible policy options?

Figuring those things out means undertaking a series of research and analytic tasks:

- Who should be involved?
  - Conduct a interest holder analysis to identify what people or groups should be involved (Who is impacted? Who has an interest? Who will influence the outcomes?). Determine when these people should be involved and to what extent.
  - Redo the interest holder analysis at every step in the process. Interest holders and their interests change as information changes and potential directions begin to take shape.
- What is the starting point?
  - Describe the challenges and opportunities presented by the issue from the perspective of the organization's purpose, values, goals, and performance.
- What else is happening in the broader context for the organization and interest holder groups that may impact the issue or potential courses of actions?
  - Conduct an environmental scan to understand other factors that may affect scope of the issue and potential policy options positively or negatively. Depending on the organization and

the issue, this might involve consideration of what's happening in any number of areas, including in the following:

- Political
- Legal
- Economic
- Social
- Technology
- Ethical
- Competition related.

- What is the real issue?
  - Separate the symptoms from the real issue.
- What is the goal?
  - Focus on the "real" issue and analyze the information collected to determine what measurable impact the policy needs to have—what needs to be achieved, maintained or avoided.
- Do the issue and related opportunities require a change in policy now that you know more?
  - Describe the current state:
    - Existing goals, strategies, and policies
    - Operational structures and high-level processes
    - Performance metrics and trends.
  - Assess the strengths and weaknesses of the current state in terms of the organization's capacity to achieve the goal without changing policy or strategy.
- What criteria will be applied to identify and assess feasible policy options. For example:
  - **Effectiveness**. The goal and targets that must be met; the impact the policy must have
  - **Doability**. Investments or compromises the organization can and is willing or not willing to make to achieve the goal (such as budget caps and risk-tolerance levels)
  - **Ethical boundaries**. Employee commitments, equity, environmental standards, targets, and more that must be met or maintained
  - **Time limits.** The time within which the policy must be fully active.

The answer to the questions in this step inform the development process. They serve to:

- Validate or reverse the decision about whether the issue or some extended form of it is significant enough to warrant assigning resources to complete the policy development process and make a change
- Set the focus and parameters of the policy development effort—narrowing and/or broadening the scope of what's necessary and/or possible and provide the criteria to identify feasible options and assess their relative value
- Inform implementation design and planning about what may need to change to operationalize a policy or what data and reporting requirements will need to be met to inform the management and evaluation functions.

Scoping and setting parameters are critical steps in the development process—they are also the steps most often skipped or underdone. Here's why.

Some leaders simply go with their gut. Others set aside time to explore the issue with their teams or set aside a day to brainstorm the scope, options, and to reach a decision with a few key internal leaders and policy people. Another group of leaders might ask the policy shop to put together background information to ensure they have "the right people" in the room for brainstorming and thinking-through of things (e.g., a interest holder analysis completed before a brainstorming session will capture different perspectives).

In our experience though, investing time and energy in this process (not going with your gut, thinking it through alone, or simply setting aside a day) is well worth it. The gut and brainstorm responses often narrow the focus to micro policy options and policies that deal with symptoms rather than issues or that deal with only part of the issue.

Fuller consideration of the smoking issue, for example, may have led organizations to a different understanding of the issue and, by extension, to different policy goals and strategies. For example, it may have ultimately led to an understanding that the complaints about smoking were actually complaints about air quality, that air quality impacts health and productivity, and that there are many elements of air quality that can be managed. This, in turn, may have led to a policy goal to improve air quality, to a policy strategy to achieve identified air-quality standards, and to implementation strategies to achieve and maintain them over time.

It would have taken more time and money in the short term to do this, but in the long term the upfront work would likely more than prove its worth. The gut/brainstorm reactors started with no-smoking policies and then developed and implemented no-scents policies, no-car idling policies, and no-vaping policies. We're guessing that the time and money it took to develop and implement all of these different policies ultimately exceeded what would have been required if they had invested more time upfront.

This approach would not have worked for COVID-19. There really was no time, and the goal, criteria, and timeline for most organizations were absolutely clear—comply with government restrictions now without negatively impacting critical goals like sustainability, production, and profit. The urgency and severity of COVID-19 were unique though. Most policy issues do not demand such immediate response, and organizations generally do have more time should they choose to use it.

Identifying Feasible Options

A feasible option is any option that, on the surface, looks like it would do what you need it to do—one that looks like it could achieve the goal affordably, efficiently, effectively, and within a reasonable amount of time. Identifying *the best* option involves identifying many feasible options and fleshing them out fully enough to assess their relative effectiveness and value.

Identifying options (feasible and otherwise) begins in the scoping step where opportunities are first identified. This can be both a blessing and a curse. It's a blessing because reasonable options have generally been identified early, and, to the extent that interest holder were engaged in the process, the organization will have some sense of the impacts and interests associated with each.

It's a curse because it can lead to anchoring and confirmation biases. Leaders and policy analysts often exit the scoping exercise with a preferred option in mind and go straight to work researching and analyzing information looking for the reasons why this option is best and the ways in which it will work.

The early assumption is that this option is the only one worth thinking about (anchoring bias), and the human tendency is then to interpret information in ways that fit with what we already think (confirmation bias). With no real comparator, there is no mechanism to challenge assumptions or to know if the option on the table is the "best" option because it is presented as the only option—or at the very least—believed to be the only "real" option.

Yes, leaders still have the authority to withhold approval, refine the policy, and send it back to the drawing board. Some leaders will do just that. They'll ask for other options. But leaders are human, too, and they often suffer from the same biases as the people they are relying on to bring them the information they need to make the best decision. Their time is limited, and if the information they receive is limited to a single option in favor of which they are already biased, their natural tendency will be to focus on this option, ask questions about, even challenge it, but they will not typically shift completely away from it.

At least two or three real and substantively different feasible options should be identified and fleshed out to enable understanding if they really would achieve the goal and meet all of the criteria identified. We say "real and substantively different" because we so often see situations where leaders are presented with the following "options":

- **Option 1**. Adopt the option as is and achieve certain outcomes
- **Option 2**. Adopt part of it and achieve a portion of what would have been otherwise achieved
- **Option 3**. Do nothing and achieve nothing

These are not three options. The first two are actually two versions of the same option, and the third has already been determined not to be viable (in the scoping exercise).

Finding real and substantively different options is not as hard as it seems. The trick is to suspend the urge to jump to an answer and understand that there is always more than one way to accomplish a goal. Reassess the information gathered in the scoping exercise and conduct a search of similar organizations and how they achieved similar goals in similar circumstances. What you are looking for is something you might reasonably expect to work and meet the criteria—options that it is reasonable to believe (based on limited information) could do the trick; that is, achieve the goal.

Even those options that people say "will never fly" could find their way to the front of the pack if they were not discarded so early. The "never fliers" aren't generally discarded because they would not be effective. In fact, over the years we have seen lots of situations where the option that would never fly was the option that policy and operational staff thought would be most effective.

These options typically get discarded because policy and operational staff assume that leaders would never go for them. That may or may not be true, but there is no way of knowing unless those options are investigated further, and the relevant information is brought forward for consideration.

The trick is to challenge the assumption that something would never fly, and you can't do that if the option is never put on the table.

Imagine the organization as a family living in the suburbs of a city with a temperate climate. There are two parents and two very active high school kids. (Perhaps even one of them has a beautiful tattoo.) Although they are all environmentally minded (they recycle and compost, try to conserve water and energy, and more), they have a 12-year-old gas-guzzling minivan they use to get to work, to the kids' activities, to the grocery store, and so on.

Most of their regular travel is within a 15-mile radius. The minivan has been in and out of the repair shop five times in the last 6 months. Their average monthly transportation costs (including gas, insurance, maintenance, and repairs) have increased over the past few years from $800 to $1,600. They are finding that the cost of running the minivan is no longer affordable and the risk and inconvenience of not having reliable transportation is escalating. The time has come. The family needs to do something different. They read the paper and listen to the news so they now know:

- The climate change situation is worsening.
- The price of gas is expected to continue to increase.
- The cost of used cars has increased significantly since COVID-19.
- The price of hybrid and electric cars is coming down.
- Governments have introduced carbon reduction policies and are actively trying to make green transportation easier and more affordable (e.g., putting in bike lanes, new transit and ferry routes, providing rebates on electric vehicles and bikes).
- Public demands for more green space and pedestrian walkways are gaining significant traction.
- Parking is becoming more and more of a nightmare.
- There are lots of new bike options (e.g., with cargo baskets that could carry groceries).
- Lots of the kids' friends are getting their driver's licenses.

They know they need to make a change in their means of transportation, and they see an opportunity (in the trends they've identified) to choose a course of action that will meet their transportation needs and be better for the environment.

They set the goals—to be able to continue to go to the places they want and need to go to and to be on time when they get there and to reduce their carbon footprint.

Together they set the criteria for the minivan's replacement:

- It has to provide a reliable means of meeting their regular transportation needs at least until the kids graduate from school and go away to college or work.
- It has to be affordable—the total monthly cost cannot exceed $1,200.
- It has to reduce their current carbon footprint by some identified amount.
- They want to be able to use the transportation when it works best for them but are willing to compromise on this to be more environmentally responsible.

The goal and criteria provide the focus for the search for feasible options.

The family identifies four options (some with sub-options).

- **Option 1**. Buy a new or used car—hybrid or electric.
- **Option 2**. Enter into a car-share agreement.
- **Option 3**. Buy bikes (electric/manual) for the parents. (The kids already have them.)
- **Option 4**. Use public transportation.

Each option is substantively different. Each has a reasonable chance of proving feasible. The next step is to determine if they all are feasible. Feasible in this case means:

- An accessible, affordable, reliable, and environmentally responsible means of enabling family members to get to where they want to go when they want to go.

Each option would be researched separately and at a high level so the family can understand more about each option as it relates to the identified goal and criteria. In this example, the research questions for each option might include:

- Will family members be able to go where they need to go when they need to go?
- How would that work?
- Is it practical? How would it work normally, in emergencies, on grocery days?
- Is it doable? Are there reputable car-sharing options available? Is public transportation available across the 15-mile radius that matters to the family?
- Is it reliable? How quickly can you access the car share? Does the bus really come every 20 minutes?
- Are there restrictions on flexibility of access and, if so, could they be managed? What are the scheduling options for car shares? What days doesn't the bus run? How nice does the

weather have to be to use a bike? Are there places it's not safe
to ride?

- Does the option meet the resource (investment) criteria?
  What are the estimated financial, energy, convenience, time,
  and opportunity costs?
- Is it green? What is the carbon footprint?

The key is to link the questions directly to the criteria and the goal.
The search is for information that decision makers would need to know to
be confident that any given option would or would not be feasible and, by
extension, would be worth spending more time fleshing out.

The answers not only provide the information required to determine
which options appear feasible, they also inform some of the conditions
under which they would be feasible and some of the requirements that
have to be met to implement them fully.

When all is said and done, there may be only one option or there
may be multiple options that are worth looking at more closely. In fact,
there often are two or more options. Sometimes what emerges out of this
process is an additional hybrid option that includes elements of two or
more of the others or something altogether different that came up and
was tested through the process.

Once you have options that are worth looking at more fully, the next
step is fleshing them out and selecting the best option.

Fleshing Out/Selecting the Best Option

This step is the last in the development process. It involves fleshing out
the remaining options to understand them in a more detailed way, to validate or invalidate their feasibility, and to inform the comparison required
to determine the best option for the organization.

Fleshing options out is about getting into the weeds. The kinds of
questions that our family would need to ask include:

- How exactly would this work?
- What challenges would be faced and how would they be
  managed?

- What exactly would have to change or be put in place to implement this option?
- What would this cost in terms of time, money, space, productivity, and so forth to implement (one-time costs) and to live it (ongoing operational, maintenance, and greening costs)?
- What benefits would be accrued when?
- What are the risks (short, medium, and long term) and how could they be mitigated?
- How do family members feel about making the change that would be required?
- What would they need to enable them to do it?

Some of these questions sound a lot like design and implementation questions. In fact, they are, and they are asked here because without the answers there would be too many unknowns to make a confident and reliable selection decision.

There are jurisdictions all over the world with legislation that has been enacted but never proclaimed and organizations everywhere with strategies and policies that were never brought to life because these questions weren't asked before the selection decision was made. In many cases those unproclaimed pieces of legislation and shelved strategies and policies are there because they proved less feasible or much more costly with a more detailed analysis. In other cases, they don't get asked until after several failed attempts to achieve the goal (witness the no-smoking policy we discussed earlier). The devil is in the details, and a high-level analysis like the one undertaken to assess general feasibility is not sufficient to uncover the realities of implementation requirements.

Fleshing out options provides the level of detail required to assess the actual feasibility of an option. It may, and often does, turn out that one or more options get crossed off the list once the detailed requirements and costs are calculated.

Those that continue to prove feasible are then compared using the detailed numbers and the additional information about benefits and risks. The comparison is conducted by looking at the variance in performance against the goal and criteria. Here, we examine and assess and compare their:

- Likely performance
- Costs (financial, level of effort, productivity dips, etc.)
- Types and levels of risk (e.g., productivity dips, disruptive trends) and the degree to which they can be mitigated
- Implementation effort and time
- Importance the organization places on an option's value add.

This last bullet refers to the value attached to additional, sometimes previously unanticipated, benefits an option brings. For example, at least two of the options identified for our transportation-challenged family would likely save them money (public transportation and bikes) and one of them would likely benefit their health and fitness (biking).

It is rare for any option to come out "first" in all the categories of comparison, and leaders often have to make hard choices or compromises (e.g., choosing the option that lowers productivity to achieve a smaller carbon footprint). It is helpful to prioritize the criteria before doing the comparison to inform these choices.

Well Developed

At the end of the day, there are no guarantees that moving through all the steps in the policy development process will produce an effective policy. Much remains to be done. This approach will, however, increase your odds of success. Here's why:

- It will result in a deliberate and better-informed, more strategic decision.
- It will decrease the need to develop multiple incremental policies to fill the gaps left by the first one.
- It will position the organization to better move through the implementation planning and evaluation pieces of the process.

- Finally, it will build confidence across the organization, in its leaders and interest holders (to the extent that they are aware of and engaged), and that policy decisions are deliberate and well thought out. This is central to the change leadership/management requirement.

And we are back where we started. Policy is not—and should not be—random. There is an accepted and effective set of practices that guide organizations from concept to completion.

Well Said

Our new Constitution is now established and has an appearance that promises permanency, but in this world nothing can be said to be certain, except death and taxes.

—Benjamin Franklin, U.S. Founding Father

CHAPTER 3

Implementation and Transition

Where the Rubber Meets the Road

A Change for the Better

Implementing new or revised policies is always about change. It's about doing what is necessary so the organization can move from the status quo to a fully operationalized policy. It's also about managing any negative impacts on the organization and on productivity in the process.

Changes take two forms:

- **Technical changes** are required to align with other policies, structures, processes, tools, facilities, and more. This alignment reinforces the policy direction given and enables and supports adoption and operationalization of the policy.
- **Human changes** align management and staff's focus, skills, expectations, and behaviors with the policy.

Successful implementations address both types of change. Indeed, the success of one enables and depends on the success of the other.

When we ask our students about the challenges their organizations face with implementation, they inevitably say "getting buy-in," and they often attach a lack of buy-in to either a lack of understanding of the specific policy or a general resistance to change. And it's true—when people don't understand something, it makes it hard to buy in, and, when people don't buy in, they will resist change.

But buy-in is a product; it is not an ingredient of effective policy implementation processes, and understanding alone is not enough to generate it. In most cases we see, the lack of buy-in occurs when organizations:

- Underestimate or ignore the level of technical change required to support and enable the policy (recall the no-smoking policy).
- Begin the effort to enable human change far too late in the process and/or rely too heavily on the distribution of the policy statement as the primary means of supporting and enabling people to change.

Some loss of productivity is common; some would even say it is inevitable, in change processes, and often the result of the following requirements:

- The need to defer operational resources to participate in elements of the development and implementation exercises.
- The time required for staff and others to process and buy into the change and to travel the learning curve associated with developing ability and competence.

That loss of productivity is often reflected using diagrams like the one in Figure 3.1 to demonstrate what happens.

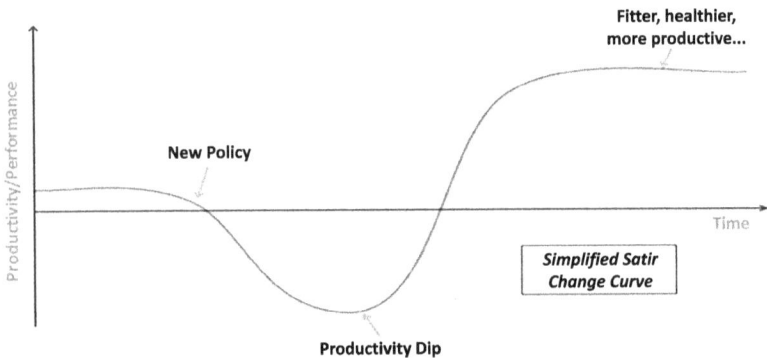

Figure 3.1 Impact of Policy Change on Productivity

The Satir Change Model was developed by Virginia Satir. The Satir Curve was originally used to describe the emotional and psychological stages people go through during change processes. It is used her to demonstrate the impact of those stages on productivity.

The goal of any policy is to reach the fitter, healthier, and more productive point illustrated on the diagram. The goal of implementation is to enable the organization to get there and to keep the depth and width of the productivity dip to a minimum while they do it.

The Technical Side of Implementation

The technical side is—wait for it—technical. The process is about identifying and making the technical changes required to support and enable (operationalize) the new policy and related behaviors and making them happen as shown in Figure 3.2.

As a process, technical implementation is straightforward:

- Identify the requirements—the future-state infrastructure.
- Identify the gaps and/or misalignment between the current-state infrastructure and future-state infrastructure.
- Design the new pieces to fill the gaps and align what's misaligned.
- Build or buy the new pieces.
- Put them in place and adopt them as the organizational norm.

The process looks like this (Figure 3.2):

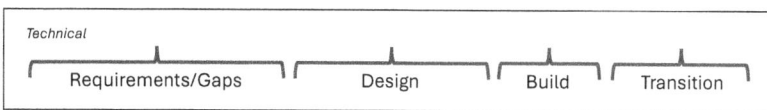

Figure 3.2 Technical Change Process

As we discussed earlier, one of the biggest mistakes we see organizations make is to underestimate the level of technical change required to support and enable new policies (and the no-smoking policy rears its head again). The organizations we are referring to often assume that communication alone will be enough to fully implement policy. This is very rarely enough. Even seemingly "simple" policies can require significant technical and human change and change strategy. The no-smoking policy, for example, resulted in requirements to change facilities, equipment, and performance management practices.

Now imagine something bigger such as remote work policies. We knew that implementing them would require many technology changes, including the purchase of more laptops to work on and software to support connectivity. We also knew that there would be changes in people's homes like finding a dedicated workspace free from distraction. And we all knew that we had no choice.

This was enough at the time. Remote work was not being implemented as a "policy" (it was not intended to be adopted as the norm); it was being implemented as a temporary emergency measure to enable social distancing during the pandemic without having to shut organizations down. No one contemplated that the measures would need to stay in place as long as they did (off and on for about 2 years) or that by the time they were no longer required to enable social distancing, many of the staff involved and many employers would see benefits to keeping the measures in place and formalizing them as policy. But that is what happened:

- Staff got used to working at home and enjoyed the autonomy, the cost and time savings, and the more relaxed dress code. They were very vocal about not wanting to return to the office.
- Employers saw opportunities to reduce facilities and equipment costs, to expand the labor pool, and to attract and retain talent at a time when the labor market was exceptionally volatile.

So now, in the post-COVID-19 era, many organizations have formalized remote work policies in place as part of their broader recruitment and retention strategies. The problem is that many of those organizations never contemplated that remote work policies would require anything additional to be effective as part of broader recruitment strategies, because they were temporary measures.

They are contemplating that now largely because cracks are beginning to show. For example:

- Leaders are worried about the erosion of shared culture and the loss of spontaneity and creative collaboration shared workspaces enable to fuel innovation.

- Managers are struggling with maintaining a sense of team and connectedness among staff, managing without a physical line of sight into what's happening on the floor, and assuring themselves that staff have appropriate workspaces, that privacy is being protected, and that staff are, in fact, working.
- Staff who are working remotely are struggling—with the blurred lines between home and work, with feeling pressure to always be available so employers won't think they're not working, and with having to work at home where there may not be an appropriate or healthy work environment.
- Staff who are working onsite are struggling with a sense of unfairness because they are not compensated for the time and money associated with traveling to the worksite.

These cracks exist because the implementation requirements of remote work policies (including those required to manage potential negative impacts) were never really fully thought through or addressed.

- Costs and benefits were never assessed relative to broader organizational criteria or compared to other options to determine whether the policies would achieve goals other than social distancing and basic productivity. (It is possible that remote work strategies are no longer aligned to achieve new organizational goals.)
- The technical and behavioral requirements to support and enable a full-fledged long-term policy were never identified or put in place.

Ideally, organizations would go back to the development process, clarify their goals, and assess what options exist and which of them (e.g., stick with remote work policy as is, reintroduce a traditional onsite work policy, or introduce a hybrid policy) is most likely to be effective given the goal and in the current and emerging environment. Some organizations are doing that now: actively reassessing the purpose of their commitment to remote work policies.

Indeed, there is significant evidence that employers are moving to abandon or change remote work arrangements. For example, in her September 11, 2023, article for CNBC, Morgan Smith says, "90% of companies say they'll return to the office by the end of 2024—but the 5-day commute is 'dead,' experts say"; she posits that "the push to get people back into offices is getting more aggressive." She cites a 2022 Korn Ferry survey of 15,000 global executives in which two-thirds agreed that corporate culture accounts for more than 30 percent of their company's market value and many leaders believe that a strong culture can only be established and maintained "if everyone is—at least some of the time—occupying the same workplace."

Some organizations are abandoning remote work policies altogether and returning to full onsite work policies bringing staff back into the office except in exceptional circumstances. Organizations like Goldman Sachs and the Federal Government in Canada fall into this category and have ordered staff back to the workplace citing the need for shared work-spaces to promote shared culture.

Many others are opting for a more balanced approach and introducing hybrid work policies with in-person work requirements. Even tech leaders like Apple and Zoom (the queen of online meetings) have reintroduced in-person work and require all staff to be in the office 3 and 2 days a week, respectively. Their reasoning is that a shared work environment enables spontaneity and enhances collaboration, creativity, and innovation—all critical elements of those companies' productivity requirements.

Regardless of the policy option chosen, it is likely more substantive technical change will be required than was originally done to implement remote work as an interim measure. The additional requirements and ef-fort might look something like this:

- ***Stick with remote work***. As the goals of remote work policies changed—the measure of their relevance and effectiveness—the technical and human changes required to operationalize them as an effective means of achieving the new goals will also have changed. Implementation work may be required to align other policies, processes, and practices like performance management, compensation, product development, and reporting to support the new goals and to enable accountability, collaboration, equity, and buy-in from leaders and managers to align things like compensation and benefits policies and performance management policies to encourage attendance and manage the risk of staff outmigration to employers with remote work options.

- *Introduce a full return to office policy.* From a purely technical perspective the effort involved might include reclaiming re-purposed space and equipment, reviewing and reversing as appropriate measures that were put in place to support remote work. It should be noted though that the primary challenge in this option would not be on the technical side of the equation.
- *Introduce hybrid policies*. With this option, organizations would need to address all the requirements to buy-in raised by the other two options.

Effective technical implementation involves changing what needs to be changed to enable the policy's effectiveness and manage impacts.

Two key questions need to be asked to understand the technical requirements and gaps:

- What organizational elements will be impacted by the introduction or continuation of the chosen policy option?
- What would need to change to manage negative impacts and to lever positive ones.

Figure 3.3 below provides an overview of what the answers to those questions might look like for those organizations that opt to formally adopt or maintain full remote or hybrid work policies. It identifies organizational elements that might be impacted.

OH and S Context

Technical
Capacity

Managerial
Line of Sight

Facilities
Requirements
and Costs

Remote Work
Impacts
Organizational
Elements

Connectivity
Opportunities
and Venues

Job
Requirements

Security Risks

Staff and
Employer
Costs

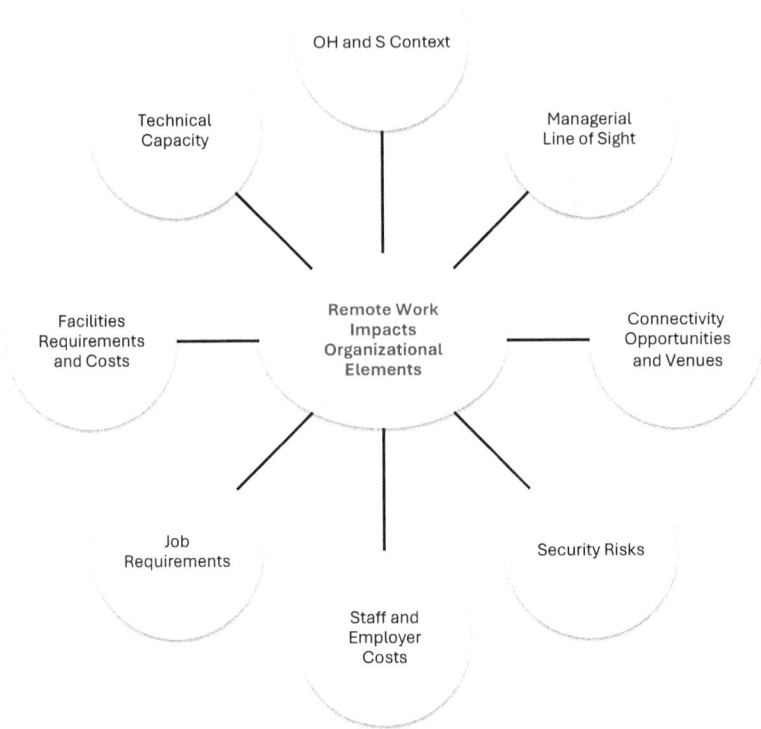

*Figure 3.3 Example of Organizational Elements That May Be
Impacted By New or Revised Remote or Hybrid Work Policies*

Once you have an understanding of what organizational elements
would need to be changed to support the new policy the design and build
steps begin. These steps are relatively straightforward.

The design process focuses on the elements that are misaligned. It
requires us to ask what the elements would have to look like and how
they would have to work to enable the policy. For example, if an organization opts to introduce or continue a fully remote work or hybrid
policy, compensation and performance management policies may need
to be changed from time and process (hours worked) to productivity and
quality standards or results to enable a greater line of sight for managers
and to strengthen accountability. Those changes, in turn, would require
technical and process changes. These should be determined and well understood before finalizing the policy decision.

The buy or build step is triggered once the policy and implementation design are approved and could involve:

- Initiating the policy review/development process to realign any policy elements identified, for example, the compensation model
- Acquiring new technologies, software, or space
- Mapping new processes to support new policies
- Training and communication to ensure everyone knows what this all means, why it's being done, and how to use the new processes and technology.

The final step in implementation is to transition the old policies, processes, tools, and other components out of use and bring the new ones in.

There are a few different approaches to transitioning. We'll focus on the ones that we see most often:

- *Big Bang Approach*. The organization picks a day, and everything goes live. Unless the technical changes involved are really minor (e.g., the removal of a step in an existing process), this approach tends to end the way it began—with a big bang. Too much too soon can lead to confusion and loss of confidence.
- *Phased Approach*. The new policies, processes, and so on are rolled out in a sequence that manages the level of change the organization needs to absorb at any given time and creates space to adjust as the changes are monitored and refined.
- *Phased/Pilot Approach*. The new processes, technologies, and so on are rolled out as said earlier, and each phase begins with a pilot project (an initial small-scale implementation) to test and validate them before they are fully implemented.

In our experience, the phased approach and the use of pilots are particularly effective. Here's why:

- It manages the level of change the organization and the people in it will need to absorb at any given time.

- It provides space and opportunity to work out bugs before full implementation and the risks that those bugs may present for productivity and quality.
- It provides an opportunity to demonstrate the validity of the change (that it can work and be effective) for those who may not yet have bought in.

The Human Side of Implementation

The human side is personal. We need to understand the technical changes in the context of personal behaviors and attachments and do what is necessary to support and enable people to be ready, willing, and able to adopt new policies.

Similar to technical implementation, the human side of implementation involves enabling a transition from the current to the future state in which the policy is fully operational. The difference is in the focus of the exercise. The technical side focuses on tangible things, things that for the most part you can see and touch, and things the organization needs. The human side, on the other hand, focuses on less tangible things including how people feel about the changes they will personally have to make and what they will need to make them - to buy into and need to participate in the change and the future state.

Take our remote work policy as an example. For staff who have been working at home for a few years and whose organizations are opting for hybrid or full onsite policies, the personal changes required may look something like what is shown in Figure 3.4 below.

As the diagram reflects, the personal impact of returning to the office for all or part of the week would have significant implications for people whose current routine and lifestyle have become dependent on working from home. The diagram would look different for staff who are already working onsite in a full or hybrid model.

Most of us don't like change—unless we believe it is worth it to us. We are creatures of habit and routine. This is what feels natural. This is what feels comfortable and safe. This is what works for us. And we don't typically enjoy having our habits and routines disrupted.

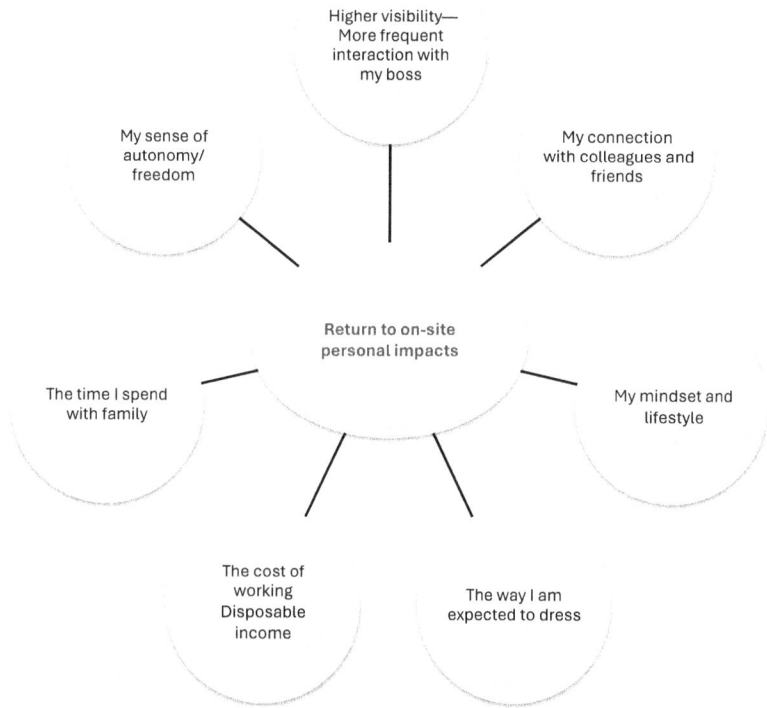

Figure 3.4 Sample Personal Impacts of Policies Requiring People to Return to Work On-Site

Most of us have a set seat at the dinner table. The place we always sit. The chair we always sit in, next to the person we always sit beside, with the view we always see. Picture a time you went in to sit down for dinner and someone (a guest perhaps) was sitting in "your" seat.

Now some of you will say that would not happen—"Everyone knows that's my seat." (That in itself is telling.) But some of you will remember a time when it did happen. What did you feel? What did you do?

If you are like most of the people we see in this situation (and we see it often on the second day of class because it doesn't take long for us to attach to "our" seats), you'll stop a little short, tense up a bit, struggle for a second or even a nanosecond before you decide to move to another chair (or ask the person in your seat to move). And then you'll spend the next few minutes feeling unhappy in your new seat (the chair isn't as broken in, the view isn't as nice, you can't reach the salt) before you settle in and feel just as comfortable as you would have felt in the seat that is no longer yours.

That tension, the hesitation, the discomfort, and the settling in, all are a natural, common, human response to change and particularly to change that you feel was not of your making. It's a process that we all go through to absorb and eventually buy into change.

William Bridges developed a model that describes the stages we move through as a curve.

We start by not accepting that the change is really happening and refusing to participate (What is he doing in my seat?! We tense up and hesitate). Then we move through a stage of suspended disbelief where we do the required thing but aren't happy about it (I found a new seat, but it's not as comfortable.) to a stage of thinking this might not be so bad after all (This seat is okay, and it has arms.) to commitment (Actually the view is just as good from this chair, and the arms actually make it more comfortable than my other chair.).

Bridges' model also describes the process we go through to adapt, the process of letting go of the way things are (reluctantly at first), giving the new thing a try (skeptically at first), and ultimately sinking into and becoming comfortable in the future state.

The human change implementation process (more often referred to as change management) is all about helping people to move through Bridges' curve. The steps look simple (Figure 3.5) and focus on enabling key states of being for people asked to change as reflected in the Figure 3.5 below.

Those states of being evolve over time and are really a product of understanding and confidence.

- Readiness (to let go) is a product of understanding two key things:
  - Why change is necessary at all/why the status quo is not an option
  - Why that should matter to me

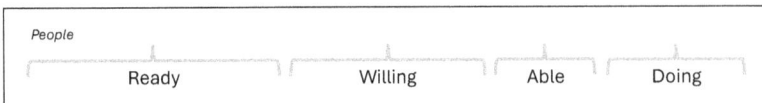

People			
Ready	Willing	Able	Doing

Figure 3.5 Human/Personal Change Management Process

- Willingness (to change and try new things) is a product of confidence in the future state, which is, in turn, a product of understanding:
  - How things will work in the future state
  - How the new things may be better for me and for my clients, customers, employees, the public
  - Why I don't have to worry about all those things I was initially worried about (the primary source of resistance)
  - What supports will be available to help me work effectively (to keep and, even better, be happy in my job) in the future state and knowing those supports will be enough
- Ability is a product of having the right tools and training and having enough time to get used to them to feel competent.
- Action is the product of feeling ready, willing, and able.

The question many organizations seem to struggle with is how to develop the level of understanding and confidence necessary to enable those states of being. The key to answering that question is in understanding that we all move through the curve, that when we begin moving through the curve matters, and that the degree to which we have had an opportunity to be privy to, involved in, and/or influence policy and policy implementation decisions will typically determine our starting point on the curve once the policy is announced.

Policy people and decision makers begin moving through the curve early. They are involved from the very beginning of the policy-making process. They have lots of time and every opportunity to become informed; to think through; to ask questions; to express and have their concerns addressed through the process; and to influence and even control the outcome. No wonder they buy in (and are so far along Bridges' curve) by the time the draft policy is shared. It's their baby. They produced it.

In organizations that struggle with buy-in, managers and technical people (those who implement changes) typically start on the curve much later. They are often engaged after the policy is already in draft form, and many of the implementation requirements are believed to have been addressed without much help, if any, from them. The same is often true for staff and other interest holders.

All too often, the first and sometimes the only opportunity these staff have to become informed, absorb, think about, ask questions, raise, and have concerns addressed is at consultation sessions where tens, sometimes hundreds, of people are invited to provide input on the draft policy.

We've all been at these sessions. A leader, consultant, or analyst spends 90 to 95 percent of the time allotted to presenting what the process has been and describing a "draft" policy and then opens the floor for the last 10 to 15 minutes for questions and feedback. That's 10 or 15 minutes to absorb and process a lot of information, to think it through, to raise concerns and have those concerns addressed and/or to provide meaningful input (the same process that the policy team and decision makers had weeks or months and multiple opportunities to move through).

To make matters worse, the presenters are usually people who have invested significant time and energy getting to this point in the policy process and are pretty sure they've got it right. This assuredness can sound much like defensiveness in consultation sessions, and defensive answers discourage dialogue.

Staff often leave "consultation" sessions like these feeling frustrated, anxious, and mistrustful. Policy people often leave thinking either "that went well" or that staff "just don't like change." The fundamental problem is that it is unreasonable to expect people who are just hearing about the substantive elements of a policy change to have anywhere near the level of confidence enjoyed by those who have been involved in its development. They are not resistant. They are confused, worried, and feeling disenfranchised.

So, what to do?

There are a number of things organizations can do to lead, manage, and enable the human/personal side of change more effectively. Some of them are truisms such as ensuring there is visible, demonstrable sponsorship, and communicate, communicate, communicate.

We'd like to focus on the two things that in our experience are most rare and most effective.

1. Undertake the policy development, technical implementation, and human change processes as an integrated process—parallel and interactive rather than linear.
2. Enable the integration by engaging managers and technical and operational staff from the beginning.

Policy Development

| Scope & Characteristics | Development and Assessment Options | Decide |

Technical

| Requirements/Gaps | Design | Build | Transition |

People

| Ready | Willing | Able | Doing |

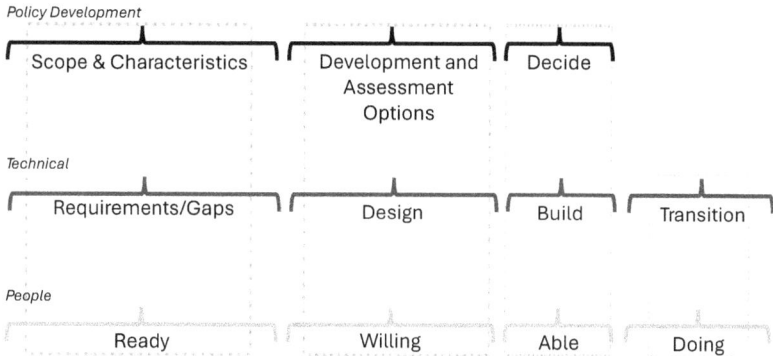

Figure 3.6 An Integrated Approach to Policy

Why would this approach be effective? Consider the diagram (Figure 3.6).

The rectangular boxes in the diagram are there to highlight the synergy between the steps in these processes. The first two boxes are where we would really like to focus your attention.

The scope and characteristics decided on in the first step of the development process provide the context and parameters for the identification of technical and human change requirements, and these requirements form part of the full scope of the policy-making effort.

The questions asked; information shared, discussed, and considered; and the thinking done through the scoping process encompass the same information and thinking that answer the questions leaders, managers, and staff need answered to reach the level of understanding required to be ready to change. The policy will also be better-informed with the addition of manager and technical and operational voices.

The development and assessment of options is all about the implementation strategy. In fact, it is the place where most of the technical design work happens, so engaging managers, technical, and operational staff here will:

- Ensure that design work is fully informed
- Enable understanding and confidence in the specific changes and in the supports that will be required for people to be willing to participate.

The decision step of the development process triggers the build process where the tools are bought and processes initiated. This is where managers and technical and operational staff are generally first engaged through communication and training processes rather than in the creative process. It positions them as receivers rather than participants in the process and the policy it produces. It is also where the training takes place to enable managers and staff to feel competent and typically when organizations begin to feel what gets characterized as resistance from staff. The reason they feel that "resistance" is because staff are still too early in Bridges' curve—their questions may not have been answered, and their worries may not have been addressed.

Transition is the point at which the organization needs people to be ready to fully adopt the change—to do the new thing and/or do things in new ways. Involving managers and technical and operational staff at the beginning of the development process enables them to move through Bridges' curve with, rather than behind, policy analysts and leaders and provides them with an opportunity to share their thinking, their thoughts, and their worries. It also provides leaders and decision makers with their best opportunity to benefit from those thoughts and ideas and to ensure that those worries will get addressed in the development of the options/ design process.

Involving managers and technical and operational staff at the beginning of the development process builds trust in leaders, the credibility of the process, and the outcome by providing:

- Staff with an opportunity to begin their personal change processes early and the opportunity for them to share their thinking and their worries when the learning is happening rather than at the end when they feel decisions have already been made.
- Leaders and decision makers with their best opportunity to benefit from feedback and to ensure that:
  - Concerns will get addressed in the development of the options/design process—the best way to achieve buy-in.
  - Scope and potential policy strategies are more fully informed—the best way to get at the root issue and the most effective strategy.

○ Implementation requirements can be more fully identified and addressed—the best way to ensure individual policies and supporting infrastructure will be aligned.

Many of our clients and students worry that real and early engagement is too time-consuming and complicated to undertake. Two things are particularly troublesome: (a) managing the logistics, time, and disruption associated with early and widespread engagement and (b) managing expectations that the outcome of the process will be exactly what every staff member thinks it will be.

The value of engagement is well documented. In the 2024 *State of the Global Workplace: The Voice of the World's Employees*, which includes data from more than 180,000 businesses in 53 industries and across 90 countries, Gallup, Inc. found that organizations with high engagement are likely to benefit from significantly higher employee well-being: reduced absenteeism (78 percent), lower turnover (58 percent), as well as higher productivity (18 percent) and profitability (23 percent) than those with unengaged teams.

According to Gallup, in best-practice organizations, engagement is built into the management work/life cycle and 75 percent of managers and 70 percent of staff are engaged.

In our experience, the logistics and effort involved can be overwhelming when organizations approach engagement as a special event that takes time out of people's schedules to organize, conduct, and attend multiple workshops and planning sessions.

However, engagement doesn't have to be so onerous. Most organizations have management structures and processes in place that can be used to build engagement in as a regular part of the management process. For example, regular management and staff meetings provide the most reliable and least disruptive venue for engagement. Making space on those agendas to discuss issues and ideas at multiple points in the policy process can be a very effective way of engaging the whole organization. This is the built-in approach that the Gallup report refers to—engagement is part of the regular course of working together or doing business.

Here's an example of what we mean. We worked with one large organization recently that adopted this approach to engage their full management and staff complement (2,000+ people) in the end-to-end policy process. Directors were asked to set aside a portion of their regular leadership meeting agendas and to table and invite their managers to discuss specific questions or conduct certain exercises (e.g., a brainstorming session) related to the topic at five different points throughout the process. And managers were asked to create space on their regular staff meeting agendas to discuss those same questions. Two of the rounds required an hour of agenda time, and the other three required only 20 minutes each.

In each case, directors and managers were provided with electronic forms to collect and submit the results of the discussions, and those results formed part of the base of information that was used directly in the decision-making process. By the end of the process when the policy was announced, there were no big surprises and there was sufficient trust in the process and the leadership to move forward smoothly.

The engagement process had not only served as a means of collecting information but had also:

- Engaged managers and staff as participants rather than receivers
- Served to keep staff informed about the organization's thinking as it moved forward
- Raised issues and ideas that may otherwise not have been raised and that did make their way into the final policy and implementation plan
- Enabled staff and managers to move through Bridges' curve with, rather than behind, decision makers and the policy team.

Taking this broad approach does not guarantee there will not be resistance later, but it does serve to reduce it significantly.

It's about managing change effectively.

CHAPTER 4

The Policy Document

Or What Everyone Calls "The Policy"

Policy exists whether you write it down or speak only of it in quiet whispers around the proverbial water cooler. Policy is known to users whether they can articulate it, lay their hands on it, or have no idea where to find the damn thing. Policy also exists in the spheres that shape, form, and guide organizations: meetings, strategic plans, town halls, speeches, annual reports, websites, mission statements, and so on. In essence, policy is what users live, breathe, and do. It is what leaders live, breathe, and do. Unfortunately, the living, breathing, and doing are not always consistent across and within groups of users and leaders. We can be out of sync with each other.

That's why we need a written policy: to document the decisions made through the development and implementation processes. This is where anyone can go to get insight into the policy, its intent, its requirements, its carrots, and its sticks. It is where users go to get answers to their questions. It is also where we often fall down. Where we stop short, ramble on, obfuscate, misspeak, and assume everyone is on the same page. They aren't.

Lack of awareness, understanding, and consistent implementation is a trifecta for policy failure. Decision making requires a strong foundation. That foundation is policy, but policy must be grounded. It must be accessible and transparent. Too often, it is neither.

Grab a pen (remember those?) and take a minute to write down everything that you think is challenging about writing policy. Answer this question: Why is policy writing hard?

Don't worry about the order of your thoughts or the neatness of your list. Just let 'er rip. Once you have your list, take a few minutes to review what you've written. Now, select the top three challenges.

See if your list matches ours. Here's what the literature tells us about writing policy. You'll notice there is an overlap with the chapter on developing policy.

First, users tell us they are confused by what policy means within their organization. This is a documentation issue from the perspective of style and formatting. If the *Respect in the Workplace Policy* bears no resemblance to the *Absenteeism Policy* that looks and reads differently from the *Occupational Health and Safety Policy*, users will have at best a conflicted sense of what policy means. At worst, they will give up trying to figure it out.

Part of this confusion comes from the myriad decision-making tools organizations have at their disposal: standards, protocols, procedures, best practices, guidelines, and so on. Policy plays a distinct and critical role. The documents that contain those policies must be readily identifiable. They must also stand alone. Inserting specific guidelines, procedures, best practices, and more in policy documents dilutes the policy. It loses focus and effectiveness.

Policies also overlap with other policies, and not usually in clear and consistent ways. This confuses users. What policy takes precedence? What if they conflict in spirit or intent? What if they are inconsistent? *What the hell am I supposed to do?* While individual policies should be designed to work in tandem with others, they often aren't.

The third challenge—and the one we'll focus on primarily in this chapter—deals with the writing in the policy document. Users are quite clear about what they think on this front.

First, they tell us we overwhelm them with information that is detailed, repetitive, and irrelevant. They get lost in the morass and can't find their way out. As a result, they guess at what we mean, or they simply give up.

Second, they accuse us of telling them absolutely nothing. Despite the plethora of words floating before them, their key questions remain unanswered. Why is this policy important? Why are we introducing this policy now? What do you want me to know? What do you want me to do?

Third, they tell us in a language we can't misunderstand and a tone that is all too clear—*I didn't understand a damn word you said.* Policy is often rooted in legalese, not the easiest of languages to learn and certainly not the most welcoming. As an important document, there is also a tendency to make the writing formal and elevated. We shy away from the everyday language of organizations that is usually understood instantly. Instead of comfortable pants and a shirt, we get dressed for the Oscars. We use the fancy word instead of the familiar one. We use six words when two will do. We use third person and distance to put a wall between ourselves and our readers. Heaven forbid we should engage them.

It is also critical to consider governance. Policy is approved at the highest levels, which means every small change will have to get sign-off. Try to put as much appropriate information in appendixes as possible so that organizational updates and routine changes to operations do not require an unnecessary and lengthy approval process.

Establishing Order

There is often a standard look and feel to policy documents across organizations. There is a structure that has been used over time and continues to be used, at least to some extent. There are two likely reasons for this. (1) The structure is helpful. It works. (2) The structure is used by others, so it must be good. Why reinvent the wheel. Add (1) and (2) together and you get this: familiarity. The document is what we expect the policy to look like, and that gives us a stronger starting point. It also enhances efficiency.

"Pick up that pen again" and write down all the sections you remember seeing in policy documents and write down all the sections you think should be there. Does your list look like this?

- Policy Title
- Policy Statement
- Scope
- Definitions
- Responsibilities
- Frequently Asked Questions
- Forms/Instructions
- Additional Contacts
- Related Information
- History
- Appendixes.

These are the most common headings in policy documents. Some are straightforward, others less so. Some are essential. Some live quite comfortably in an appendix. Let's dive in.

Policy Title

The title gives users important information in a few words. It identifies the key purpose of the policy, highlights the group to whom the policy applies, and helps to distinguish the policy from others with similar names and content. For example, if we are an elected official, we know the "Code of Conduct for Municipal Employees" is not the document we want. But we know we're headed in the right direction.

The plain-language movement and the desire to engage readers have led to the development of creative titles. A round of applause to the authors of "Fantastic Yeasts and Where to Find Them: The Hidden Diversity of Dimorphic Fungal Pathogens"; "Medical Marijuana: Can't We All Just Get a Bong?"; and "Gut Microbe to Brain Signaling: What Happens in Vagus...."

Policy documents have resisted the urge to be clever, to be cute, to be creative—and with good reason. The policy document is a reference tool. No one sits down with a chilled glass of wine in front of a roaring fire and settles in to savor a 60-page policy. When we have a question we turn to the policy document, much like we use a thesaurus when we're looking for a synonym or a dictionary when we want to be sure what a word means. Finding information is faster when we know we have the right document at hand.

We've been talking about COVID-19 policies in organizations. Workable Technology Limited offers a number of sample templates companies can use as a starting point for writing these policies. They include titles like *Coronavirus (COVID-19) company policy* and *COVID-19 mandatory vaccination and workplace safety policy*. Nothing fancy. Not a chuckle in sight. But if you're looking for information, you'll know whether your questions are likely to be answered.

Policy Statement

The policy statement is a common starting point for many policy documents. It's also named "Purpose" and, in some cases, "Introduction."

THE POLICY DOCUMENT 65

Regardless of what it is called, the policy statement serves to spell out the strategy the policy is linked to, the goal of the policy, who is affected by the policy, and a high-level overview of the policy. The policy statement is not the place to provide background details about the policy or procedural steps. As with elsewhere in the document, it's best to avoid specific labels and names that often change, such as software products and designated employees.

The policy statement also sets the tone for what is to follow. With this in mind, it is an ideal spot to espouse a value for your organization and to identify the benefits of the policy for users and the organization itself.

Here is an example of a COVID-19 policy statement out of the UK. It appears to be a template. (We found at least two companies that are using this language, Dechert LLP, a global law firm, and Baxall Construction Limited.)

Protecting the health and well-being of our employees, contractors and anyone affected by our work is our top priority and we have developed a proactive plan designed to minimize the impact of COVID-19 within our workplace. We will implement the plan in phases as necessary, commencing immediately, following guidance from Public Health England and the UK Government. The COVID-19 public health emergency guidance is constantly changing. Therefore, this policy and our management plans will be subject to change and ongoing reviews. All changes to the policy will be communicated to employees by e-mail, company intranet and posted on company notice boards.

The policy includes the measures that we are actively taking to protect our employees, visitors and contractors from the COVID-19 virus and to further mitigate the spread of it through the company and wider community.

To maintain a healthy and safe workplace, all employees and contractors are requested to follow all the rules diligently. It is important that we all act responsibly and transparently to these health precautions.

If you take a close look at the statement, you'll notice it opens with a value statement: We care about the people we work with. It goes on to reinforce that value by highlighting how employees will be kept informed of changes. It ends by showing how everyone benefits—with a healthy and safe workplace.

Also pay attention to the tone. It sounds businesslike but approachable. Too often policy documents come across as stuffy or pompous, heavy-handed or distant. That does not encourage further reading. It certainly doesn't foster buy-in.

Scope

Not all policies apply to all employees or all customers or all suppliers. This section lets users know whether they need to pay attention to this document, whether it will impact what they do or how they do it. It also defines the type of content as well as the type of user. Take a look.

In its online discussion of open access policy, the Canadian Association of Research Libraries provides a number of samples of this section, all dealing with the same issue. You'll see how divergent the section can be.

- All UPEI scholars, including, but not limited to, staff, faculty, graduate and undergraduate students. (University of Prince Edward Island)
- We commit to deposit all scholarly articles authored or co-authored while we are university authors at SFU, although this policy does not cover any articles published before the adoption of this policy, any articles for which the author entered into an incompatible licensing or assignment agreement before the adoption of this policy, or any articles published after we leave the university. (Simon Fraser University)
- The University relies on its researchers to uphold principles of scholarly rigor so that open materials are of the highest

research quality and, where appropriate, will aid reproducibility. This may include:

○ Where possible, ensuring all publications are Open Access

○ Where appropriate and possible, "making openly available the underlying data relating to these publications

○ Sharing protocols openly

○ Collaborative approaches including blogging, online editions, releasing teaching materials, pre-print deposit." (University of Cambridge)

In its COVID-19 policy, Baxall Construction Limited, a UK company, says:

Scope

This coronavirus policy applies to all our employees who are either working in the office or at home. It is imperative that those personnel working from home read through the working from home guidance notes to ensure we maintain a collective and uniform response to this challenge.

Definitions

The "Definitions" section is not intended to define every key word in the document. It clarifies the meanings of important terms and those words that have a specific meaning for the purpose of the policy (but that may be defined differently in other contexts).

Policies often contain language that may be specific to the organization or industry, and definitions help ensure that everyone interpreting the policy understands its terms in the same way. This can help prevent misunderstanding, confusion, and misinterpretation that could lead to noncompliance or other issues. By providing clear definitions up front, a policy can also be more effectively communicated and implemented across an organization.

Here is the section from the Cowichan Tribes COVID-19 policy.

POLICY DEFINITIONS

2.1. In the COVID-19 Safety Policy:

- Chief and Council refers to the thirteen duly elected members that make up Chief and Council.
- Directors and/or Managers refers to the employees of Cowichan Tribes who are formally assigned to manage a department and/or program.
- Employees refers to all persons employed by Cowichan Tribes.
- Employer refers to Cowichan Tribes.
- Frontline worker refers to employees who are delivering services in community members' homes or interacting directly with the public.
- Household refers to individuals who live in one house.
- Immediate supervisor refers to employees who have designated responsibility for directly managing and overseeing the work of other employees.
- Occupancy limit refers to the maximum number of persons allowed in a room. Signage outside and inside the room will indicate the occupancy limit, which is determined by Directors and/or Managers in consultation with the COVID-19 Project Manager, taking into consideration multiple factors including but not limited to how much space is available to accommodate the physical distance of 2 meters/6 feet between each person.
- Person refers to both employees of Cowichan Tribes and nonemployees.
- Self-isolation refers to staying home, not having visitors in your home, avoiding contact with others in your home, and keeping a physical distance. Self-isolation also includes hygiene and cleaning protocols such as wearing a mask and/or face shield when around others, washing your hands regularly, and disinfecting commonly touched surfaces.
- Social distancing or physical distancing refers to maintaining two (2) metres/six (6) feet distance between persons.

- Work from Home Agreement refers to the written agreement between Cowichan Tribes and an employee, which is prepared by the immediate supervisor, Director and/or Manager in consultation with the Human Resources department and signed by the employee.

The "Definitions" section can get quite specific and quite lengthy. Be rigorous. Does a word really need to be defined, or will it be commonly interpreted in the way the document intends? That said, we need to make sure we don't assume everyone will interpret a word the way we do.

The biggest debate about this section is where to place it: at the beginning or at the end? While there is no consensus on the "right" answer, there is general agreement that the longer the "Definitions" section, the better it is to place it near the end of the document so that it doesn't distract from the heart of the policy discussion.

This issue, of course, is of greater concern when the policy document is printed. Online versions can dispense with a "Definitions" section in favor of hyperlinking a word to the definition or revealing the definition when the mouse rolls over it.

Responsibilities

Also often called "Roles and Responsibilities," this section serves a crucial purpose in clearly defining the duties, authority, and expectations of individuals or entities involved in implementing the policy. Its content typically includes:

Role Definitions

This outlines the various roles involved in the execution of the policy and spells out who is responsible for what tasks. For example, it might reference roles like "Administrator," "Supervisor," "Employee," or "Compliance Officer." The intent is to ensure clarity and accountability.

This section also assists with efficiency. Users, for instance, will typically seek out the role that belongs to them. Unionized employees might read this one section and safely skip the part intended for nonunionized employees.

Responsibilities

Each defined role is accompanied by a list of specific responsibilities that outline what each role must do to ensure compliance with the policy. Here's an example for a COVID-19 policy:

1. Leadership Team:
   - Develop and communicate clear COVID-19 policies and procedures
   - Provide necessary resources and support for policy implementation
   - Lead by example in adhering to safety protocols
   - Monitor and adjust policies as needed based on evolving circumstances
2. Employees:
   - Adhere to all COVID-19 policies and procedures outlined by the organization
   - Follow health and safety guidelines, including wearing masks, practicing proper hand hygiene, and maintaining physical distancing
   - Promptly report any symptoms of illness or potential exposure to COVID-19 to designated personnel
   - Cooperate with contact-tracing efforts if necessary
   - Stay informed about updates to policies and guidelines
3. Human Resources and Health and Safety Personnel:
   - Provide guidance and support to employees regarding COVID-19 policies and procedures
   - Facilitate training sessions on proper safety protocols
   - Manage requests for accommodations related to COVID-19
   - Coordinate with relevant authorities for testing, contact-tracing, and other health-related matters
   - Maintain confidentiality regarding employees' health status
4. Facilities Management:
   - Implement and maintain sanitation protocols for common areas and high-touch surfaces
   - Ensure proper ventilation in indoor spaces

- Arrange seating and workspace layouts to facilitate physical distancing
- Provide necessary supplies, such as hand sanitizers and tissues, in accessible locations
- Regularly inspect facilities for compliance with health and safety standards

5. Security and Compliance Personnel:
   - Monitor adherence to COVID-19 policies and procedures
   - Enforce mask-wearing and physical-distancing protocols as necessary
   - Assist with crowd control and capacity management in shared spaces
   - Report any violations or concerns to appropriate authorities
   - Collaborate with HR and management to address noncompliance issues

6. Communications Team:
   - Disseminate timely and accurate information regarding COVID-19 policies, updates, and resources
   - Address common questions and concerns from employees
   - Coordinate internal communications channels to ensure consistent messaging
   - Monitor external sources for relevant developments and adjust communications strategies accordingly
   - Foster a culture of transparency and trust through open communication channels

7. External Partners and Contractors:
   - Adhere to the organization's COVID-19 policies and procedures while onsite
   - Communicate any relevant health and safety concerns to designated personnel
   - Comply with any additional requirements or protocols established by the organization
   - Collaborate with internal teams to maintain a safe working environment for all parties involved

Authority

Here, the extent of authority each role possesses is described. It delineates decision-making powers and limits, ensuring that actions are taken within the scope of the policy and relevant regulations, including, for example, but not limited to, the following:

1. Leadership Team:
   - Holds ultimate authority for decision making regarding COVID-19 policies and procedures
   - Empowered to allocate resources and make strategic adjustments to the policy as needed
   - Responsible for communicating policy updates and expectations to all stakeholders
2. Human Resources and Health and Safety Personnel:
   - Authorized to interpret and apply COVID-19 policies in accordance with legal requirements and organizational needs
   - Granted the authority to enforce policies, including disciplinary action for noncompliance, in collaboration with the management
3. Facilities Management:
   - Authorized to implement and enforce facility-related COVID-19 protocols, including sanitation measures and physical-distancing guidelines
   - Empowered to make adjustments to facility layouts and operations to ensure compliance with health and safety standards
4. Security and Compliance Personnel:
   - Granted authority to monitor and enforce compliance with COVID-19 policies, including mask-wearing and physical-distancing protocols
   - Authorized to intervene in situations of noncompliance and escalate issues to appropriate channels as necessary
5. Communications Team:
   - Authorized to disseminate information regarding COVID-19 policies, updates, and resources to all stakeholders

- Granted authority to communicate on behalf of the organization regarding COVID-19-related matters, ensuring consistency and accuracy in messaging
6. External Partners and Contractors:
   - Expected to comply with the organization's COVID-19 policies and procedures while onsite
   - Required to follow instructions from designated personnel regarding health and safety protocols
7. Legal and Compliance Advisers:
   - Consulted for guidance on legal requirements and implications related to COVID-19 policies and procedures
   - Authorized to provide recommendations on policy adjustments to ensure compliance with applicable laws and regulations

Reporting Structure

This section may also detail the reporting relationships among different roles—not specific people. It specifies to whom individuals should report for various matters, facilitating effective communication and problem resolution. This may work well in an appendix.

Applicable Standards

This section, which may also work well as an appendix, might outline any training or education requirements for individuals assuming specific roles. This ensures that personnel are adequately prepared to fulfill their responsibilities under the policy.

Monitoring

Monitoring, including for compliance, is always a tricky issue in policy documents. It can't—and shouldn't—be avoided, but taking central stage makes the policy sound heavy-handed and puts the focus on enforcement, not engagement. The "Responsibilities" section may describe how compliance with the policy will be monitored and evaluated. It may include measures such as audits, assessments, or performance reviews to ensure adherence to the established roles and responsibilities. Highlighting why such compliance is critical is always helpful.

If we were to create a "Roles and Responsibilities" section for an early COVID-19 policy, it might look like this:

Management Team

The management team is responsible for overseeing the implementation of this COVID-19 policy and ensuring compliance with all relevant regulations and guidelines. They are tasked with making strategic decisions regarding workplace safety measures, resource allocation, and communication protocols.

Employees

All employees are required to adhere to the guidelines outlined in this policy to mitigate the spread of COVID-19 within the workplace. Responsibilities include practicing proper hygiene, wearing face coverings as mandated, maintaining social distancing, and reporting any symptoms or exposure promptly.

Human Resources

The HR department is responsible for providing guidance and support to employees regarding COVID-19-related policies and procedures. They oversee the implementation of workplace accommodations, such as remote work arrangements or flexible scheduling, for vulnerable individuals or those requiring quarantine.

Health and Safety Officers

Designated health and safety officers are responsible for monitoring compliance with COVID-19 safety protocols and conducting regular risk assessments. They ensure that appropriate measures are in place to protect employees, visitors, and customers from potential exposure to the virus.

Facilities Management

Facilities management is responsible for implementing and maintaining physical-distancing measures, sanitation protocols, and ventilation systems to reduce the risk of COVID-19 transmission within the workplace. They oversee the regular cleaning and disinfection of shared spaces, high-touch surfaces, and common areas.

Communication Coordinators

Communication coordinators are responsible for disseminating timely and accurate information regarding COVID-19 updates, policy changes, and safety guidelines to all stakeholders. They ensure that employees are aware of their responsibilities and are kept informed of any developments related to the pandemic.

Compliance Officers

Compliance officers are tasked with monitoring and enforcing adherence to COVID-19 policies and procedures. They investigate reports of non-compliance, address any concerns raised by employees, and implement corrective actions as necessary to maintain a safe working environment.

Plain language teaches us that a picture can be worth a thousand words. The same is true of illustrations, graphs, and charts. The information about general responsibilities could be presented like this for easy and quick identification of the appropriate role and the reading of the information related to that role:

Role	Responsibilities
Management Team	• Oversee implementation of policy • Ensure compliance with all relevant regulations and guidelines • Make strategic decisions regarding workplace safety measures, resource allocation, and communication protocols

Employees	• Adhere to the guidelines outlined in this policy to mitigate the spread of COVID-19, including the following:
	  ○ Practicing proper hygiene
	  ○ Wearing face coverings as mandated
	  ○ Maintaining social distancing
	  ○ Reporting symptoms or exposure promptly

Frequently Asked Questions

This section is relatively new to policy and still somewhat controversial. There are those who contend FAQs are an add-on to assist understanding and use of a policy—but they belong outside the policy document itself. Others point out, if the FAQ section is helpful—and often used—then it belongs in the policy document itself. Putting FAQs inside the document increases the chances the information will be read and the policy understood.

There's nothing mysterious, obscure, or complicated about FAQs. We see them daily: on websites, in reports, or as attachments to procedures. The key is to be substantive without being overwhelming. If you honestly feel there are 248 questions related to a policy, group these questions so that answers can be located quickly and easily. That's the whole purpose of FAQs: boiling the policy down to key questions you know users will want answered.

Here are some potential questions that might appear in a COVID-19 policy FAQ section:

- What safety measures are being implemented to prevent the spread of COVID-19?
- Do we need to wear masks while at work? If so, are there specific guidelines for mask-wearing?
- What is the protocol for reporting COVID-19 symptoms or exposure?
- Are there any resources or support for COVID-19 testing?
- What should I do if I test positive for COVID-19?
- Are there any changes to the sick leave or remote work policies due to COVID-19?
- How often are high-touch surfaces and common areas sanitized?
- What should we do if we encounter a coworker not following COVID-19 safety protocols?
- Are there travel restrictions or guidelines for employees who need to travel for work?

- What support is offered for employees struggling with the mental health effects of the pandemic?
- Are there any resources available for employees who need assistance with childcare or eldercare due to COVID-19 disruptions?
- What measures are in place to protect vulnerable or high-risk employees?
- Will personal protective equipment (PPE) such as gloves or face shields be provided?
- What happens if an employee refuses to comply with COVID-19 safety measures?
- How will we be updated on any changes to the COVID-19 situation or policies?

These next sections appear straightforward, even a tinch boring. They might be both. That doesn't make them irrelevant or unimportant.

Forms/Instructions

Ensuring easy access to relevant forms and necessary instructions:

- Provides clear direction to employees on how to properly complete any necessary forms related to the policy
- Ensures employees understand what information is required and how to provide it correctly
- Helps make sure employees have easy access to the necessary documentation and are more likely to comply with the policy's requirements
- Promotes consistency and standardization by providing uniform forms and instructions for all employees to follow
- Reduces the likelihood of errors or discrepancies in how the policy is implemented
- Saves time and effort for employees who need to access the information

- Creates a paper trail that can be used for documentation and recordkeeping, which can be valuable for tracking compliance, conducting audits, or addressing any disputes or issues that may arise.

If the policy is available online, this could be a link to the forms that are found at the end of the policy document for ease of use, but not part of the policy document itself. For hard copies, the forms could be an appendix.

Additional Contacts

This can be a pain-in-the-butt section. It's often nitpicky, uninteresting, and time-consuming. And it matters. Here's why:

- Additional contacts provide a readily accessible list of people users can reach out to for assistance or clarification regarding the policy.
- It may include individuals or departments with specialized knowledge or authority related to the policy's subject matter.
- This section clarifies who within the organization is responsible for handling inquiries or issues related to the policy.
- It may include information on higher-level contacts or escalation procedures helping to ensure a clear path for addressing more complex or serious matters.
- Emergency contact information, such as numbers for security personnel, emergency response teams, or external agencies, may be found here.

Again, this does not have to be part of the core policy document.

Keep in Mind

Nothing is going to change as quickly as a list of names, titles, and contact info. This can easily make a policy out of date and frustrating to use. Where possible, try to avoid specifics. For instance, use "Director of HR," instead of "Diana Prince, Director of HR."

Related Information

Like most of these backend sections or appendixes, this is about being helpful and making it easier for users to find information and get answers to their questions. Here's how the "Related Information" section does that.

- It provides additional context and background related to the policy's subject matter. This, in turn, helps users understand the rationale behind the policy and the factors that influenced its development or implementation.
- The section may include references to relevant laws, regulations, or industry standards that inform or support the policy. This lets users better understand the legal or regulatory framework within which the policy operates.
- In cases where the policy is linked to or intersects with other organizational policies or initiatives, the "Related Information" section may highlight these connections. This paints the bigger picture. It enables users to see how the policy fits into the broader framework of organizational policies and goals.
- Here users will find links or references to supporting documentation, such as guidelines, procedures, or best practices, that complement or expand upon the policy's requirements. This gives access to additional resources for understanding and implementing the policy effectively.
- The "Related Information" section may contain links to training materials or resources designed to help employees understand and comply with the policy.

History

In all likelihood, this will be a brief history and included as an appendix. What goes here is the record of significant changes to the policy listed in chronological order. This information will be helpful to those administering and overseeing the policy. For users, it shows a commitment to policy. Or a lack of one.

Appendixes

Information that is nice to know but not essential to know goes here. This section often links to lengthy or complex documents that provide additional or supplemental details. In the case of a COVID-19 policy, there might be copies or links to government documents or websites outlining COVID-19 regulations, recommendations, and requirements. There might also be a link to procedures for maintaining a safe workplace.

Well Said

Now your policy has a structure. It's time to settle on a language. You have two choices: formal and conversational. Guess which one most organizations use? Guess which one readers prefer? Guess who's winning the debate?

Here are two possible openings for a COVID-19 policy.

Formal

In light of the ongoing global pandemic caused by the novel coronavirus (SARS-CoV-2), our organization has formulated a comprehensive COVID-19 policy aimed at mitigating the transmission of the virus within our premises, ensuring the safety and well-being of our employees, clients, and stakeholders while simultaneously adhering to the guidelines and directives provided by relevant public health authorities and governmental bodies.

Conversational

Due to the COVID-19 pandemic, we've created a policy to keep everyone safe. This policy follows health guidelines to prevent the spread of the virus among our employees, clients, and visitors.

Which opening do you prefer? Why? It's the latter question that is most important. As policy writers, we need to understand what resonates with our users, what works for them, and why it works for them. Then we replicate that approach across all our policies.

It's clear what opening is easiest to read. That would be the conversational paragraph. We'll talk more about readability scores in the chapter on communicating policy, but for now, let's take a quick look at how each of these paragraphs fare when put through a readability formula.

Formal

Flesch readability score: 15.1 (Equivalent to a grade level)
Reading ease: 41.7 (Or how many people out of 100 would understand this paragraph easily the first time they read it.)

Conversational

Flesch readability score: 8.1
Reading ease score: 55.9

It can be difficult to let go of technical language, legalese, and the terms common to an organization or profession. We worry that we'll sound less educated, less knowledgeable, and less expert. There is also a belief, waning rapidly, that elevated language is more impressive. Here's a grammatically correct sentence:

In the realm of understanding, it has been cautioned against forming conclusions based solely on the external presentation of a tome, emphasizing the depth and richness that lie within its pages, often hidden from plain sight.

What does this mean to you? If you were to explain this to a 7-year-old, what would you say? Chances are you would translate some of the more unfamiliar language into everyday words. You'd likely rewrite the sentence in your mind to be sure you have the meaning correct. Policy readers are tired of deciphering text. They'd rather we simply said:

Don't judge a book by its cover

There has been a decided and definitive move toward plain language. Indeed, this preference for language that is understandable and usable has become a demand from the public. Many organizations are listening. So are government and regulators. In fact, President Barack Obama made clear government communication the law more than a decade ago when the *Plain Writing Act of 2010* was enacted.

Plain language is common sense. It means readers (and listeners) are more likely to understand the information being conveyed and act accordingly. From a policy perspective, language that is familiar, content that is concise, and information that is complete result in better decisions and better performance. Not to mention enhanced compliance. (Plain language is discussed in more detail in *The Thong Principle: Saying What You Mean and Meaning What You Say*.)

Plain language may be easy to read, easy to understand, and easy to use. It is not easy to write. It can take time, practice, and commitment to write in a way that is both professional and clear. The results make it worth the effort.

Try your hand on these training examples from Medicaid and available on the plainlanguage.gov website.

Original

The Open Door Initiative is a program based on a simple and fresh attitude: that the CMS desires to better hear and interact with those beneficiaries, providers, and other stakeholders interested in the delivery of quality health care for our nation's seniors and beneficiaries with disabilities. This increased emphasis on responsiveness is captured through an ongoing series of 'Open Door Forums that provide a dialogue about both the many individual service areas and beneficiary needs within CMS.

Flesch–Kincaid Grade Level = 22.21
Flesch Reading Level = 4
(We'll talk more about what these numbers mean in a few pages. For now, suffice it to say, this is a difficult sentence no matter how many PhDs you have.)

Before you look at the rewritten version, take a minute to identify what about the earlier paragraph that doesn't work for you. What could cause readers to scratch their heads, to have their eyes glaze over, to wish they were anywhere but here?

Rewritten

We want to hear from you!

Help us improve our service to you. Attend an Open Door forum near you. For information about upcoming forums, visit cms.gov.

Flesch–Kincaid Grade Level = 4.6
Flesch Reading Level = 73.3

You'll notice instantly the difference in length. You'll also notice the latter sounds like a human being is speaking. Readers make it quite clear they do not want to interact with a department, a company, or an agency. They want to communicate with a person, and if writing sounds cold, indifferent, and distant, readers will assume that reflects the approach and nature of the organization.

One more example. This one reflects another element of plain language and one that is critical to clear, easy-to-use policies.

Original

Medicaid: Apply if you are aged (65 years old or older), blind, or disabled and have low income and few resources. Apply if you are terminally ill and want to receive hospice services. Apply if you are aged, blind, or disabled; live in a nursing home; and have low income and limited resources. Apply if you are aged, blind, or disabled and need nursing home care, but can stay at home with special community care services. Apply if you are eligible for Medicare and have low income and limited resources.

Flesch–Kincaid Grade Level = 9.3
Flesch Reading Level = 61.0

Now close the book for a minute and take a stab at rewriting this. Welcome back. Here's the revised version:

You may apply for Medicaid if you are:
- Terminally ill and want hospice services
- Eligible for Medicare and have low income and limited resources

- 65 years old or older, blind, or disabled and have low income and few resources and:
  - Live in a nursing home
  - Need nursing home care but can stay at home with special community care services

Flesch–Kincaid Grade Level = 6.3
Flesch Reading Level = 69.0

The first thing that strikes you is the formatting. Charts, boxes, lists, and bullets have been fixtures in policies for decades. They make it easier to read, locate, and interpret information. This emphasis on visual readability is growing and evolving.

The front page of the TD Bank Group's 2023 *Code of Conduct and Ethics for Employees and Directors* (available online) does not look like a typical policy. There is no white cover page with black text. No diving into the details.

Instead, the cover page is a photo of what we assume are contented bank employees. The only other text on the entire page aside from the title: Thank you for your efforts in protecting our reputation as a trusted financial institution.

It's about readability, and about putting a human face on policy.

Inside you'll find a few other anomalies. First, there is a message from the group president and CEO and the board chair. It's intended to make policy more than mere words—to make it about people—and to underscore the importance of the document, which is why this is a technique you would not use for every policy. The E-mail-Use Policy does not need endorsement from senior leaders.

Following the message from management is—wait for it—a table of contents. How radical. How helpful.

This 21-page corporate policy, while text-heavy, attempts to make the text less dense and repetitive with the use of color and images. For online policies, these are no-cost options that carry big benefits.

Ultimately, a policy document works because users can understand it and act accordingly without having to set aside several hours and purchase a new thesaurus. Ultimately, a policy document works because users can find themselves in the document. They understand why the policy is important—to them and to the organization they work for.

CHAPTER 5

Communicating About the Policy

Or What Everyone Thinks Happens When They Write the Policy Document

As we've mentioned throughout this book, policy is a spectrum of activities that come together and stand apart to help you develop and implement policies that are effective. That spectrum starts with developing the policy and then it moves to writing the policy document. As you read in the previous chapter, the third stage is ensuring the organization is ready for the change that will follow in the wake of a new and revised policy.

Now it's time for the fourth phase on the spectrum: communicating the policy. This can be as simple as sending an e-mail to announce that a new or revised policy is ready for users to review. It can be as complex as engaging users throughout every step of the policy development and implementation process. And everything in between.

What communicating policy is not: a checklist. There is no standardized to-do list that spells out how, when, and where to communicate about a policy. The reason for that is simple. Not every policy is the same. Not every organization is the same. Not every user group is the same.

We wouldn't use the same grocery list week in and week out. What we need in the summer is not necessarily what we need in the winter. We may have company coming for a visit, and the meals we dish up will change (at the very least, quantities will be larger). We may celebrate certain holidays with special menus. We may even need to go to stores we don't usually shop at.

That said, there are staples on a grocery list. The bread and butter, as it were, of ensuring a home is well stocked with food. The same is true of policy. There are tools and techniques that are commonly used to create awareness and enhance understanding of the policies in our organization. We'll look at those staples as well as other techniques to ensure policy is being interpreted as intended.

Let's start with why we bother to communicate about policy. The document is approved. It's posted. Now it's up to users to do their due diligence. We can wash our hands of this policy and move on to the next one.

Aah, if only life were so simple.

We can't move on, but we can move forward—and that requires informing users about the policy and involving them to the extent necessary and possible. When we do that, we have users who can perform better because they have a strong framework for decision making. And we have much more.

Communicating about policy increases knowledge and understanding. It enhances compliance. It reinforces, across the organization, the importance of policy and helps to build bridges, manage expectations, and engage users. Communication also helps us to build a policy culture—the policy culture we actually want.

We'll talk more about this later. First, let's think about what confounds us about communicating policy and how not communicating sends an important message. Take a moment to jot down the challenges you've faced when it comes to communicating policy in your organization. If you haven't yet had to communicate about policy, try to imagine what those challenges might be.

Chances are your list will be as long as ours. We've got six items we'd like to discuss with you. Topping our list: controlling the message.

"Control" is a tough word and one that we often shy away from. In this context, it refers to staying on top of the message, getting ahead of the grapevine, and avoiding surprises. Surprises are fun when it's your birthday, not so much when you're talking about a policy.

It's important to remember that control is nuanced. First, we want to ensure that understanding of the policy among users mirrors our own understanding of the policy. If the intent of our COVID-19 policy is to give employees the option to work from home—but users conclude they have no choice but to work from home—then what we have here is a disconnect.

Such disconnects can be significant. We recently conducted an evaluation of an orientation program for a government department that helps families in crisis. As part of that evaluation, new employees were asked what they would do in a specific situation. We got three broad categories of responses. When we asked the employees—all committed, reliable, productive individuals—why they would act as indicated, we were told by everyone, "It's in the policy."

We shared these responses with their supervisors—all committed, reliable, productive individuals—and asked them what they thought. They applauded their new employees for doing the right thing. When we asked how they knew it was the right thing, they said, "It's in the policy."

We can all read the same words and get very different messages. Communicating about a policy before, during, and after its implementation can help to avoid divergent interpretations and practices.

In addition to building a unified understanding of what the policy says, communication also helps to ensure we all perceive the purpose of the policy in the same way and the intent behind its requirements. For example, we may see our COVID-19 policy as a health and safety support for employees. They may see it as a means to force vaccinations on them. We need to avoid such disconnects as much as we possibly can.

Policies can also be detailed and complex. They can be controversial and sensitive. These realities can be difficult to navigate. One e-mail will not do it. More is required often before there is even a final policy.

Next on our list: timing. Get users involved and informed too late in the process and they feel like policy is being imposed on them. They have no input even when the policy directly affects them. This small flame of resentment burns much brighter if there are elements of the policy that do not make sense, are difficult to comply with, or will mean changing the way people work.

Timing is also linked to control in the sense of who gets to talk about the policy first: the organization or the users. Being first out of the gate is important. It lets you build the foundation on which future discussions will be based.

Organizations understand why a policy is necessary and why it is being implemented now. Users know a policy will affect them. Until they see or hear the policy, however, they do not definitively know what that effect will be. They may worry. They may be annoyed. At the very least, they will be talking. That talk can be detrimental to an organization, especially if the assumptions being made and the information being conveyed are not accurate.

Organizations decide when a policy will be released (although laws and regulations may dictate a deadline for that release). Where possible, and it usually is, policy should be released when the waters are calm. Not that long ago, for example, there was a controversy sparked by an airline that refused to let two teenagers on a plane because they were wearing leggings. In the midst and wake of that public debate it would not be a good time to introduce a dress code policy.

Policy can be perceived as top-heavy and authoritative. Trying to see past this can be difficult for users, and this difficulty poses a challenge for organizations issuing a new or revised policy. Policy is most effective when the need for the policy and the value it brings to the organization are evident to those who developed the policy and those who must live with it.

Communicating policy also requires resources: human and financial. Depending on how lengthy the development process and how significant the rollout, there can be distribution costs, travel expenses, printing bills, IT-related expenditures, and more. Not to mention employee time, energy, and effort. These costs must be weighed against the benefits of a recommended communications plan. It may be that the plan needs to be scaled back.

Finally, users tell us, repeatedly, that communicating about policy is sporadic in their organization. They do not know how to interpret this. Did someone forget? Is one policy more important than another? Can some policies be ignored? Can policy generally be ignored? Consistency is critical to ensuring organizations build the policy culture they want for their organization. Communications cannot be ad hoc or irregular.

Why Bother?

Clearly, communicating about policy takes thinking and effort. Everyone is busy; the to-do list is long. So why bother? Why not just let users know there is a new policy and leave it to them to read the policy and reach out if they have any questions?

Here's why. Consistently (and effectively) communicating about policy:

- Increases knowledge and understanding
- Enhances compliance
- Helps build the policy culture you want
- Reinforces the importance of policy
- Identifies next moves
- Builds bridges
- Helps manage expectations
- Engages users.

Times Have Changed

How we communicate in organizations has changed and with good reasons. The times have changed. That includes technology, of course, but the way we work has also changed.

Douglas McGregor, a renowned management professor at MIT, proposed two contrasting theories about workforce motivation and management in his 1960 book *The Human Side of Enterprise*. These theories, known as Theory X and Theory Y, describe two different views of individuals and the implications for managerial behavior and communication.

Theory X

Assumptions:

1. **Inherent Dislike for Work:** Employees inherently dislike work and will avoid it if they can.
2. **Need for Control:** Because of this dislike, most people must be coerced, controlled, directed, or threatened with punishment to get them to put forth adequate effort toward the achievement of organizational objectives.
3. **Avoidance of Responsibility:** Workers prefer to be directed, wish to avoid responsibility, have relatively little ambition, and want security above all.

Communication Implications:

1. **Top-Down Communication:** In a Theory X environment, communication tends to be more directive and top-down, with managers giving orders and employees expected to follow them without input.
2. **Limited Feedback:** Feedback from employees is often minimal because their opinions and suggestions are not highly valued or sought.
3. **Formal and Rigid:** Communication structures are more formal and rigid, emphasizing control and adherence to set procedures.
4. **Focus on Compliance:** Emphasis is placed on compliance and adherence to rules rather than collaboration or innovation.

Theory Y

Assumptions:

1. **Work as Natural as Play:** Work is as natural as play or rest, and people will exercise self-direction and self-control if they are committed to the objectives.
2. **Intrinsic Motivation:** Employees are motivated by the desire to achieve, and they seek out responsibility under the right conditions.
3. **Capacity for Creativity:** People are imaginative and creative in solving problems, and their intellectual potential is only partially utilized in most organizations.
4. **Commitment to Objectives:** If employees are committed to the objectives, they will work toward them without the need for external control or punishment.

Communication Implications:

1. **Two-Way Communication:** In a Theory Y environment, communication is more likely to be two-way, with a focus on dialogue and feedback. Managers seek input from employees and encourage their participation in decision making.

2. **Open and Informal:** The communication style is more open and informal, fostering an atmosphere of trust and mutual respect.

3. **Encouraging Innovation:** There is a greater emphasis on encouraging creativity and innovation, with employees feeling more valued and engaged.

4. **Empowerment and Responsibility:** Communication often focuses on empowering employees, delegating responsibility, and recognizing their contributions, which enhances motivation and job satisfaction.

In the 1980s, Dr. William Ouchi, an American professor and author, continued this thinking in his book *Theory Z: How American Management Can Meet the Japanese Challenge.* It combined the best aspects of American and Japanese management styles, emphasizing a strong company culture, long-term employment, and collective decision making. Ouchi's Theory Z aims to create a work environment that enhances employee loyalty and job satisfaction, leading to improved productivity and performance.

Theory Z

1. **Long-Term Employment:**
   - Promotes job security and encourages long-term commitment from employees.
   - Employees feel more secure and invested in the company's success.

2. **Collective Decision Making:**
   - Decisions are made through consensus, involving employees at all levels.
   - Encourages collaboration and a sense of ownership among employees.

3. **Individual Responsibility:**
   - While decisions are made collectively, individuals are responsible for their implementation and outcomes.
   - Balances teamwork with personal accountability.

4. **Slow Evaluation and Promotion:**
   - Emphasizes gradual career progression based on comprehensive evaluation.
   - Reduces pressure and competition, fostering a more cooperative work environment.
5. **Holistic Concern for Employees:**
   - Management shows genuine interest in the well-being of employees, including their personal lives.
   - Creates a supportive and caring work environment.
6. **Integrated Organizational Culture:**
   - Strong company culture that aligns with the values and goals of both the organization and its employees.
   - Ensures that everyone works toward common objectives.

Implications for Communication

1. **Enhanced Employee Engagement:**
   - **Two-Way Communication:** Encourages open dialogue between management and employees. Employees are more likely to share their ideas and feedback.
   - **Active Listening:** Management practices active listening, valuing employee input and fostering a culture of mutual respect.
2. **Collaborative Decision Making:**
   - **Consensus Building:** Communication is geared toward building consensus, requiring transparent sharing of information and collective discussion.
   - **Inclusive Meetings:** Meetings and discussions include representatives from various levels, ensuring diverse perspectives are considered.
3. **Strong Organizational Culture:**
   - **Cultural Communication:** Emphasis on communicating the organization's values, mission, and vision regularly to reinforce the company culture.
   - **Rituals and Symbols:** Use of organizational rituals and symbols to build a sense of community and shared purpose among employees.

4. **Holistic Communication:**
   - **Personal and Professional Support:** Communication goes beyond professional matters to include support for personal well-being, indicating a genuine concern for employees' overall happiness.
   - **Mentorship Programs:** Establishing mentorship and support programs to guide employees in their career and personal development.
5. **Long-Term Focus:**
   - **Strategic Communication:** Focus on long-term goals and strategies in internal communications, aligning daily tasks with overarching objectives.
   - **Continuous Feedback:** Regular, constructive feedback that emphasizes long-term improvement and development rather than immediate results.
6. **Trust and Loyalty:**
   - **Transparency:** Transparent communication practices build trust and loyalty. Employees are kept informed about important decisions and changes within the organization.
   - **Open-Door Policy:** Encourages an open-door policy where employees feel comfortable approaching management with their concerns and suggestions.

Bottom Line

The way we work has changed. Therefore, the way we communicate has had to change. This applies to policy.

Then and Now

Traditionally, communication has been about dispensing information so that employees will know how to do their jobs and understand what is expected of them. Informing policy users meant disseminating facts, using data, and translating experience. The focus was on creating *content* so that policy users could *learn*.

Organizations shifted from this communications approach to interesting users in the information. This involved using anecdotes and examples and ensuring information was relevant to the user. The focus was on creating *context* so that policy users could *understand*.

Fast forward to today. Communication relies on all the elements used to inform and interest readers, but it goes beyond that to involving them, to making their policy culture experiential. The focus is on *engagement* so that policy users will *remember*.

Audience Analysis

Communication starts with the first of the five Ws: who. We need to know who will be using this policy. That knowledge must be detailed.

Specificity is critical. If we are a hospital and we want to reach health care professionals in our organization, "health care professionals" as a target audience will not do it. Do we mean doctors? All doctors? Specialists? Surgeons? Nurses? Continuing care assistants?

Drilling down into our audiences enables us to understand the breadth and depth of users. It also begins the process of determining how to best reach these potentially diverse groups.

We usually start with four main groups:

- Primary audiences
- Secondary audiences
- Internal audiences
- External audiences

Primary audiences are our main targets. These are the people who we need to reach, who need to know and understand this policy. These are the people we also need to know how to reach. (This is not as easy as it sounds.)

Secondary audiences are just that. While it is helpful to inform and engage them, it is not necessary. It is nice for them to know; it is not necessary.

External audiences bring a unique set of challenges. They do not necessarily share the same knowledge as internal audiences, and a different tone and greater detail may be required in communicating with them.

Internal audiences share common ground even if the work they do is significantly different. They also often share an organizational language.

Sometimes it's obvious what audiences belong in what groups. Often, it isn't. For example, are partners and consultants internal or external audiences? Also, a target group can be a primary audience for one policy and secondary for another, for example, a board of directors.

Key Messages

Once we know who needs to receive our communication, we need to determine what we want to say. In part, this will reflect the audiences we are reaching out to. In part, it will underscore what we want these audiences to know and remember about the policy we are discussing.

Communicating policy goes far beyond attaching the policy document and saying, "Happy reading." It is not a summary of the policy. It is not a frequently asked question (FAQ) pasted in the body of an e-mail. Successful communication lets audiences know why this policy is important and why they should pay attention to it.

The starting point is developing key messages. These are the main points you want your audiences to know. If they learn nothing else, if they remember nothing else, they must know this.

Key messages are written from the users' point of view. Consider what is most important in their minds and get right to the point. Deliver critical information without wasting your audience's time and energy with unnecessary details.

Not only will your key messages be short. There will also not be many of them. Three is a recommended number. This allows you to focus in on central points.

Often key messages have three components. First, there is the foundational statement, which highlights the one thing you want your audiences to know or understand about this policy. Second, there may also be supplemental points that support the main statement. This might be a statistic, a reference to another organizational document, or a timeline. Finally, there is the human face to your policy. This is why the policy matters—and why the policy should matter to your users. It could be a quote, it could be an intro from a peer, or it could be an endorsement of the policy of a champion in the organization

How About That?

So now we know who we are communicating with and what we want to say to them. It's time to think about how we communicate.

Inclement Weather Policy, Diversity Policy, and Dress Code. These are three different policies—and three different types of policies. How would you communicate information about these policies before they are implemented, as they are being rolled out, and after they are implemented?

Let's start where the policy starts—with an idea, with a need, with a decision. From here, policy moves to research, conversation, and analysis. The policy is taking on life. What could you do to engage users of these three policies? What should you do? Some things to consider.

Chances are you'll spend more time communicating with users of the latter two policies at the development stage. For the inclement weather policy, it might be helpful to give a shout-out to managers to alert them to the new policy being developed and ask for input. Perhaps they could add this to their staff meeting agenda and garner feedback. If appropriate, you might want to sit down to chat with union reps. Of course, if the organization operates 24/7 or is an essential service, you may want to engage managers, frontline staff, and outside workers more fully.

The inclement weather policy is an organizational policy. It does not usually come with the concerns, questions, or emotional responses that other polices, such as diversity and dress codes, bring with them. A diversity policy is a value-laden policy. These are relatively new in the world of policy, and it could be argued that the policy is not necessary from a decision-making point of view. It is from the perspective of letting users and the rest of the world know what you stand for as an organization. Engagement of users will be critical.

This is the kind of policy where it may be helpful to establish a working group or advisory group that can lead the process and speak on behalf of that process as the policy takes form and shape. In keeping with the theme of the policy, the advisory group should be led by a member of an equity group, one who will spearhead communication and give credibility to the process.

The same approach may be helpful for the dress code, a controversial policy you know will get pushback even before it is developed. A working group, preferably led by a frontline staff person, can serve to temper emotions and enhance listening. We are often much more willing to be respectful and attentive to someone who is not a member of the leadership team but rather a peer.

As policies develop, ongoing communication is often helpful. In the case of the inclement weather policy, you may wish to circulate a draft in advance for comment on whether the document is understandable and whether there are any unanswered questions. This fosters engagement. It also helps to solidify thinking and identify any issues with the policy in advance of implementation. For policies like the diversity policy and the dress code, ongoing communication may be beneficial throughout the development process. This may include town halls, staff meetings, e-mails, intranet postings, and inclusion in speeches or talks from senior management. What drives the communication plan will be both the organizational importance of the policy and the anticipated response from users.

Once a policy is developed, it needs to be rolled out. This can be as simple as sending an e-mail to all users with a link to the policy. This might work for the inclement weather policy. It might also work for the dress code if the development process engaged users. The diversity policy will require more. Going beyond the ordinary underscores both the importance of a policy and the need for users to review it carefully. In the case of a diversity policy, a more noteworthy rollout also builds support for the policy.

Policies like diversity can be launched at an event, managers can devote part of staff meetings to reviewing the policy, and/or there can be posters to announce the new policy. Senior leadership should be visible and vocal. You might also wish to bring in others from outside the organization who work in this field to say a few words or share a piece of cake.

Once a policy is officially implemented, communication doesn't end. Policies need ongoing reminders. In the case of the inclement weather policy, an e-mail before the first predicted snowstorm of the season would be appropriate. It could remind users of the policy, include the FAQs, and include a wish for everyone to stay warm and safe.

The diversity policy might take on a higher profile. It could be mentioned in the annual report and included on the organization's website. Here though is an opportunity to show how policy is lived. Users from diverse groups could be pictured online, profiled in the employee newsletter, or featured in the annual report. This isn't about referencing the diversity policy per se; it is about showing how the organization has embraced the policy.

The dress code policy requires a softer touch. No fanfare. This is where managers play a key role. If policy is a standing item on the staff meeting agenda (and it should be), the dress policy could be mentioned as summer approaches and wardrobes change. It, like the diversity policy, should also be part of the orientation for new employees.

A communications plan to guide policy-related activities is recommended. This doesn't have to be long or complex. It can be as simple as a checklist; nevertheless, for more significant and controversial policies, it will need to be more detailed.

How Do They Do It?

In 2018, the European Union introduced a new General Data Protection Regulation throughout Europe. As a result, companies had to update their privacy policies. Many companies, such as Fitbit and Google, took this opportunity to update their privacy policies generally and beyond the continental borders of Europe. In the following boxes, you'll see communications from four companies—Fitbit, Google, Pinterest, and Norwegian Reward (Norwegian Air's free customer loyalty program). They differ in length, content, and approach (Figures 5.1–5.3).

Figure 5.1 Fitbit Privacy Policy

At Fitbit, our goal is to help you lead a healthier, more active life by empowering you with data, inspiration, and guidance to reach your goals.

We're updating our *Privacy Policy* and *Terms of Service* to support our latest products as well as upcoming changes to European data protection law. We're also introducing new and improved account settings to provide all of our customers with more control over their data. Here are some of the key updates:

Greater transparency. We appreciate that you are trusting us with information that is important to you. We want you to understand how and why we use your data and how you can control that use. Our updated *Privacy Policy* more clearly describes our data practices, like our data retention, and how you can use your account settings to manage your data.

More control. We have enhanced the settings we give you to control your data. With these improvements, it is easier for you to edit or delete personal data you have given us, like your profile data; control how your personal stats and other information are visible to other Fitbit users; download your information, including data about your activities, body, foods, and sleep; control the notifications you receive from us; and manage the third-party apps you have authorized to access your account.

New products. The *Privacy Policy* updates support our new software features, including the addition of female health tracking to our Fitbit app and smartwatches, and the introduction of family accounts where parents can set up accounts for their children to use with select Fitbit devices, as described in our *Privacy Policy for Children's Accounts*.

Our European operations. We updated our *Terms of Service* to reflect our global business. If you live in the European Economic Area, United Kingdom, or Switzerland, Fitbit International Limited, an Irish company, will provide you with the Fitbit services and control your personal data. This update does not affect the services we provide you. If you reside elsewhere, your service agreement remains with Fitbit, Inc., a U.S. company.

Please read the updated *Privacy Policy* and *Terms of Service* in full. By using our services on or after May 24, 2018, you'll be agreeing to the revisions, unless you accept them sooner, such as when you agree to them while creating an account or pairing your Fitbit device with your account. You can review the previous versions in our archives *of previous privacy policies* and *terms of service*.

Thanks for your interest in Fitbit!

Figure 5.2 Google Privacy Policy

Google   caenman1@gmail.com

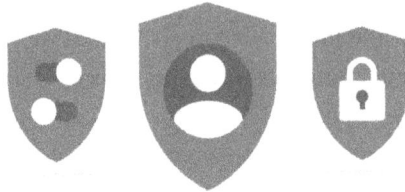

This month, we're updating our Privacy Policy to make it easier for you to understand what information we collect and why we collect it. We've also taken steps to improve our Privacy Checkup and other controls that we provide to safeguard your data and protect your privacy.

Nothing is changing about your current settings or how your information is processed. Rather, we've improved the way we describe our practices and how we explain the options you have to update, manage, export and delete your data.

We're making these updates as new data protection regulations come into effect in the European Union. and we're taking the opportunity to make improvements for Google users around the world.

We're making these updates as new data protection regulations come into effect in the European Union. and we're taking the opportunity to make improvements for Google users around the world.

Making our Privacy Policy easier to understand

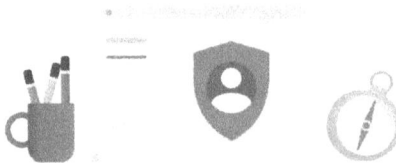

Simpler structure & clearer language

We've improved the navigation and organisation of the policy to make it easier to find what you're looking for. We've also explained our practices in more detail and with clearer language.

New descriptive videos & illustrations

Often a visual description is easier to understand than text alone, so we've added short videos and illustrations throughout the policy.

Embedded privacy controls

We've made it easier to jump to key settings directly from the policy, helping you make choices about your privacy.

Improving your privacy controls

Within the past year, we updated My Activity so that you can better access and manage the data in your Google Account. We also launched a redesigned Dashboard, which allows you to easily see an overview of products that you're using and your data associated with them.

This month, we've updated our Privacy Checkup with new illustrations and examples to help you make more informed choices about your key privacy controls. And since we understand that your preferences may change over time, the new Privacy Checkup enables you to sign up for regular reminders to check your privacy settings.

To learn more about these and other controls to manage your privacy, visit your Google Account.

Google

© 2018 Google LLC, 1600 Amphitheatre Parkway, Mountain View, CA 94043

Figure 5.3 Pinterest Privacy Policy

Updates to our Privacy Policy

Thank you for using Pinterest!

Here's a preview of the new Privacy Policy that'll go live on May 1, 2018.

Our mission is to help you discover and do what you love. To do that, we show you personalized content and ads we think you'll be interested in based on information we collect from you and third parties. We only use that information where we have a proper legal basis for doing so.

We wrote this policy to help you understand what information we collect, how we use it and what choices you have about it. Because we're an Internet company, the following concepts are a little technical, but we've tried our best to explain things in a simple and clear way. We welcome your *questions and comments* on this policy.

We collect information in a few different ways:

1. **When you give it to us or give us permission to obtain it**

   When you sign up for or use Pinterest, you give us certain information voluntarily. This includes your name, e-mail address, phone number, profile photo, Pins, comments, and any other information you give us. You can also choose to share with us location data or photos. If you buy something on Pinterest, we collect payment information, contact information (address and phone number) and details of what you bought. If you buy something for someone else on Pinterest, we collect their delivery details and contact information.

If you link your Facebook or Google account or accounts from other third-party services to Pinterest, we also get information from those accounts (such as your friends or contacts). The information we get from those services depends on your settings and their privacy policies, so please check what those are.

2. **We also get technical information when you use Pinterest**

Whenever you use any website, mobile application or other Internet service, certain information gets created and logged automatically. The same is true when you use Pinterest. Here are some of the types of information we collect:

Log data. When you use Pinterest, our servers record information ("log data"), including information that your browser automatically sends whenever you visit a website, or that your mobile app automatically sends when you're using it. This log data includes your Internet Protocol address, the address of and activity on websites you visit that incorporate Pinterest features (like the "Save" button—more details in the following text), searches, browser type and settings, the date and time of your request, how you used Pinterest, cookie data and device data. If you'd like, you can *get more details* on the types of information we collect in our logs.

Cookie data. We also use "cookies" (small text files sent by your computer each time you visit our website, unique to your Pinterest account or your browser) or similar technologies to capture log data. When we use cookies or other similar technologies, we use session cookies (that last until you close your browser) or persistent cookies (that last until you or your browser delete them). For example, we use cookies to store your language preferences or other settings so you don't have to set them up every time you visit Pinterest. Some of the cookies we use are associated with your Pinterest account (including information about you, such as the e-mail address you gave us) and other cookies are not. For more detailed information about how we use cookies, please review our *Cookies Policy*.

> **Device information.** In addition to log data, we collect information about the device you're using Pinterest on, including type of device, operating system, settings, unique device identifiers and crash data that helps us understand when something breaks. Whether we collect some or all of this information often depends on what type of device you're using and its settings. For example, different types of information are available depending on whether you're using a Mac or a PC, or an iPhone or Android phone. To learn more about what information your device makes available to us, please also check the policies of your device manufacturer or software provider.
>
> 3. **Our partners and advertisers share information with us ...**
>
> *The e-mail continues for six pages.*

Compare this communication to the one from Norwegian Reward (Figure 5.4).

Figure 5.4 Norwegian General Data Protection Regulation

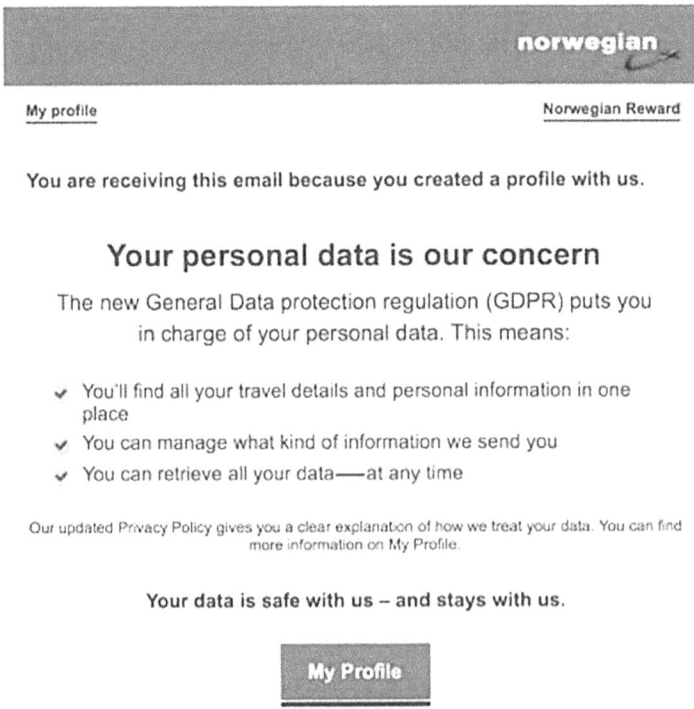

My profile   Norwegian Reward

You are receiving this email because you created a profile with us.

Your personal data is our concern

The new General Data protection regulation (GDPR) puts you in charge of your personal data. This means:

- ✓ You'll find all your travel details and personal information in one place
- ✓ You can manage what kind of information we send you
- ✓ You can retrieve all your data—at any time

Our updated Privacy Policy gives you a clear explanation of how we treat your data. You can find more information on My Profile.

Your data is safe with us – and stays with us.

My Profile

Steeped in Culture

Every organization has a policy culture. It may not, however, be the policy culture they want. Policy doesn't just happen (at least it shouldn't). The culture in which policy lives and breathes in your organization shouldn't either.

Policy culture refers to the set of values, beliefs, attitudes, and practices shared by members of an organization regarding the development, implementation, and adherence to policies. It is how an organization collectively perceives and engages with its policies, reflecting the organization's commitment to governance, compliance, and ethical standards. A strong policy culture ensures that policies are not just documents but are actively integrated into daily operations and decision-making processes.

Creating a robust policy culture involves several strategic steps:

- *Leadership commitment.* Leadership must demonstrate a commitment to policies by not just adhering to them but also by communicating their importance. Leaders are also expected to model compliance and ethical behavior. This demonstrates from the top-down that policies apply to everyone.
- *Clear and accessible policies.* If policy is truly important, it must be transparent. This includes ensuring that policy documents are clear, jargon-free, and easy to understand. Policies also need to be accessible, and this includes ongoing communications.
- *Employee involvement.* Involving employees in the policy development process increases buy-in and relevance. Establishing channels for employees to provide feedback on existing policies and suggesting improvements is recommended.
- *Education and Training.* Where appropriate, training programs can help to educate employees about policies, their importance, and their application. Refresher courses can keep employees updated on any policy changes or new policies.
- *Communication.* What we've been discussing throughout this chapter. Regular outreach through various communication channels keeps policies top of mind. Also essential: fostering

an environment where employees feel comfortable discussing policies and seeking clarification.

- *Integration into daily operations.* We discussed this in the previous chapter. Embedding policies into daily operations is essential. So is ensuring that policy considerations are a part of the decision-making process at all levels of the organization.
- *Monitoring and enforcement.* There is a carrot and a stick when it comes to policy. Both have a role to play. Regularly monitoring adherence to policies, often through audits and reviews, sends a message to users about the importance of policy. And as difficult as this is to do, applying policies consistently across the organization helps avoid perceptions of favoritism or bias.
- *Recognition and accountability.* Carrot: Acknowledge and reward employees who exemplify strong adherence to policies. Stick: Hold employees accountable for policy violations with fair and transparent disciplinary processes.
- *Continuous improvement.* Organizations need to periodically review and update policies to ensure they remain relevant and effective. They also need to be open to change and willing to revise policies in response to feedback or changing circumstances.

CHAPTER 6

Monitoring and Evaluation

More Than a Gut Feeling

Policy monitoring and evaluation provide a structured approach to tracking and measuring progress and performance and to assessing the effectiveness, efficiency, and impact of your policies. They aren't just things that are nice to do. They are necessary. There is no point in developing, writing, implementing, and breathing life into policy if you then don't bother to find out if it's working. And there's the rub. What does "working" mean? We'll get to that. First, let's all agree that monitoring and evaluation are essential. Here's why.

Effective policy is about more than compliance (because yes, you can have 100 percent compliance with a policy that is getting you nowhere). Monitoring and evaluation are a strategic means of supporting decision making, promoting continuous improvement, and informing future planning. When organizations monitor and evaluate policies, anything really, it moves them closer to meeting objectives. These functions help organizations to stay on track and remain agile, to adapt to changing circumstances, and to ensure long-term success. This is particularly relevant here because, as we've discussed, policy is broad. It isn't just one document that sits on a shelf, digital or otherwise.

"Monitoring" and "evaluation" are similar. The terms are often used interchangeably, and, in fact, monitoring is a type of evaluation. Both involve the analysis of data to inform decision making and both provide organizations with insight about whether they're on track and about what is working and what isn't. There are some key differences though.

Monitoring is conducted on a regular and ongoing basis and is used:

- To track operational and organizational progress and performance data, to ensure things are functioning well and that the organization is headed in the right direction; and
- To inform short-term operational decisions about things like process or resource allocation, adjusting as required to stay on track.

Evaluations, on the other hand, are time-bound, deeper dives conducted periodically to demonstrate accountability (retrospective) and to learn about and assess the overall value or effectiveness of policy and to inform decisions about the policy itself and the future course of action (prospective).

They get triggered when:

- A predetermined evaluation date arrives. This is generally set to align with and inform decisions about contract or funding renewals and so on;
- The data that are tracked and reported regularly suggest the organization is not progressing or performing well over time; or
- There is a significant development or change in the industry or policy environment.

Evaluations generally apply both retrospective and prospective lenses. With the retrospective lens, we're looking back to see how well we did, however we define "well." Many of you will be familiar with this type of evaluation. It can look like this. Assume we have a remote work policy, and we want to assess its impact. We could compare productivity metrics such as project deadlines from those who work remotely and those who don't, or from before and after the policy was implemented. If we're hopeful that offering the option to work remotely will boost employee satisfaction and reduce turnover, we can conduct quarterly employee satisfaction surveys and compare turnover rates before and after the policy's implementation.

The notion of prospective evaluation is a little more difficult to grasp. It's about looking forward. In the case of policy, this type of evaluation assesses the link between an organization's policy intentions and the relative value of the policy options under consideration. It seeks to anticipate the impact of policy before it is implemented. For example, in their article, "Action-Oriented Prospective Policy Analysis to Inform the Adoption of a Fiscal Policy to Reduce Diet-Related Disease in the Solomon Islands," Erica Reeve et al. were assessing the development and implementation of a tax on sugar-sweetened beverages (SSBs). They conducted a prospective policy analysis, including document analysis and qualitative interviews with key interest holders, a quantitative analysis to frame the policy problem and examine appropriate implementation mechanisms, and economic modeling to outline the potential benefits associated with different proposed policy solutions. "Our analysis demonstrated that SSBs were being consumed in relatively large amounts, especially by children, and that there were likely to be substantial health and economic benefits associated with an SSB tax."

The following table highlights key differences between monitoring and evaluation:

Element	Monitoring	Evaluation
Focus	Short Term—Inputs, process, and outputs	Long Term—Outcomes, impacts, and results
Scope	Operational progress and organizational performance	Policy value and effectiveness
Purpose	Track progress and improve implementation	Assess overall value and inform future policy
Methodology	Regular data collection and reporting	In-depth analysis and assessments
Data	Real time	Historic and real time
Frequency	Continuous cycle—daily, weekly, and monthly	As required or triggered and time-bound

The monitoring side of this equation seems to be more intuitive to organizations. Monitoring frameworks are developed and actioned as a regular part of doing business. Virtually every organization we've worked with or read about has some form of regular reporting framework and process.

On the evaluation side, organizations also seem to be relatively comfortable with and adept at *program* evaluation, but things get a bit murkier when it comes to *policy* evaluation. Policy evaluation assesses policies. It does not assess individual programs linked to those policies.

Policies exist to support organizational purpose and goals that are generally defined at a "macro" level. The strategies undertaken to achieve those goals often involve the development and implementation of numerous sub-policies and programs or interventions. This can make the measurement and attribution of effectiveness difficult.

Why Bother?

There are many reasons why evaluation is important. Topping the list is determining whether a policy has achieved its intended outcomes. This helps organizations decide whether to continue, revise, or discontinue a particular policy.

Policy evaluation is also about accountability. Organizations have a fiduciary duty to their stakeholders—employees, investors, citizens, or customers—to ensure that policies are implemented effectively and deliver measurable results. Evaluating policies also helps organizations manage risks, make improvements, plan for the future, and demonstrate they are meeting their obligations.

Bottom Line

Peter Drucker said it best—"You can't manage what you don't measure."

Monitoring and evaluation data collection and reporting requirements should be identified in the development process and built into reporting structures and processes as part of implementation. This enables the production of the reports and analyses (including evaluations) to inform operational and future policy decisions. Analysis feeds decision making.

This will sound obvious. It isn't.

Knowing how evaluation plays a key role in ensuring effective policies are in place is important. Equally important, knowing what should be evaluated. That would be:

- Policy options, decisions, and implementation strategy;
- Implementation and change management processes;
- The changes made and the impact they have;
- The effectiveness of the direction given.

Types of Evaluation

Organizational policy evaluation typically falls into three categories: developmental, process, and outcome evaluation. Each is used at different stages of the policy lifecycle depending on the goals of the organization.

- *Developmental evaluation*: This occurs during the development phase of a policy. Its primary purpose is to assess the potential effectiveness of different policy options and offer up insight before full implementation. For example, a company rolling out a new training policy for leadership development may conduct a evaluation to assess delivery methods before selecting a final approach. This is a prospective evaluation—what is likely to happen.
- *Process evaluation:* Process evaluation focuses on how well a policy has been implemented and is operating. It examines whether the implementation followed the original plan and identifies obstacles or deviations. For instance, a process

evaluation of a sustainability policy would assess whether the organization successfully implemented energy-saving measures, such as LED lighting and improved insulation, and whether employees were adequately trained in energy conservation practices. This is a retrospective and real-time analysis.

- *Outcome/impact evaluation*: This type of evaluation assesses the overall effectiveness of a policy in achieving its intended outcomes well after implementation. For example, if an organization introduces a wellness policy aimed at reducing absenteeism, an outcome evaluation would measure whether employee absenteeism rates, in fact, decreased and whether the decrease was caused or enabled by the policy action. This is a retrospective analysis—what happened.

But wait. It can also be prospective. If the initial outcome analysis shows the policy has been effective, you then need to assess if the policy is likely to continue to be effective. If the policy is found to be ineffective, the question "why" can be explored.

Let's Process This

Policy evaluation, like most evaluations, has specific requirements. Key among these are:

- Information about the Policy including
  - Its measurable objectives
  - Its defined criteria
  - Key indicators and targets
- Baseline data
- Credible, strong sponsorship
- Assumptions
- Objectivity.

Once you have the requirements in place, or at least included in the process, it's time to dive in. Figure 6.1 below provides an overview of the

Set Focus & Scope	Select Methodologies	Develop Tools	Gather Data	Conduct Analysis	Decision-making

| • Purpose
• Criteria
• Logic Model
• Stakeholders
• Evaluation / Questions | • Data Requirement
• Collection Plan
• Logistics Plan | • Existing Reports
• Specific Questions
• Surveys | • Pre-test
• Data Collection | • Qualitative
• Quantitative | • Interpretation
• Report
• Action Plan |

Evaluation Framework	Methods & Plan	Data Collection Tools	Data	Finding	Decisions

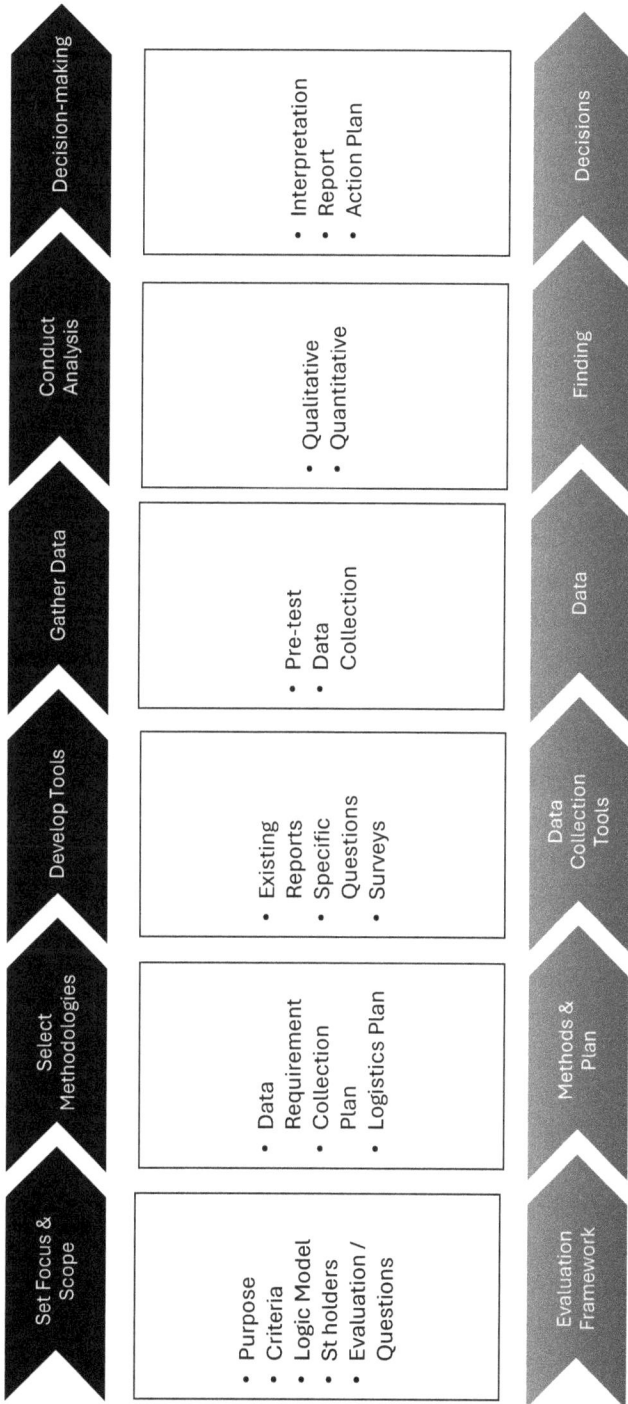

Figure 6.1 Evaluation Process, Key Components and Deliverables

steps in the evaluation process, and the key elements and the deliverables in each step:

The scoping step is about getting clarity:

- To understand why the evaluation is being done and how the answers will be used:
  Ask: Who is asking for the evaluation?
      Who is the key audience?
      Who are the key interest holders?
- To understand what you are evaluating:
  Ask: What is the key question being asked?
      What criteria will be applied to assess the answer?
      What indicators will be tracked to provide measurable answers?
      What targets will mark the difference between success and
          something other than success?
      What is the baseline?
- To understand what is being evaluated:
  Ask: How was the policy supposed to work?
      What was it supposed to accomplish?
- To understand what the evaluation needs and its limitations:
  Ask: What kinds of information will be needed?
      Where is information available?
      From whom is it available?
      When is it required?
      What resources are available to collect it?
      How much time is needed?

One tool to help you visualize and answer some of the framework questions is a logic model (Figure 6.2). This lays out how the policy is intended to work—the desired impacts and results—given the key assumptions that have been made and the broader organizational considerations.

Together, the answers to these questions form an *evaluation framework* to focus and guide you through the process. More than that though, the framework provides focus and clarity to the policy development and implementation processes—the better you understand it when the policy development process begins, the better the policy and its implementation will be.

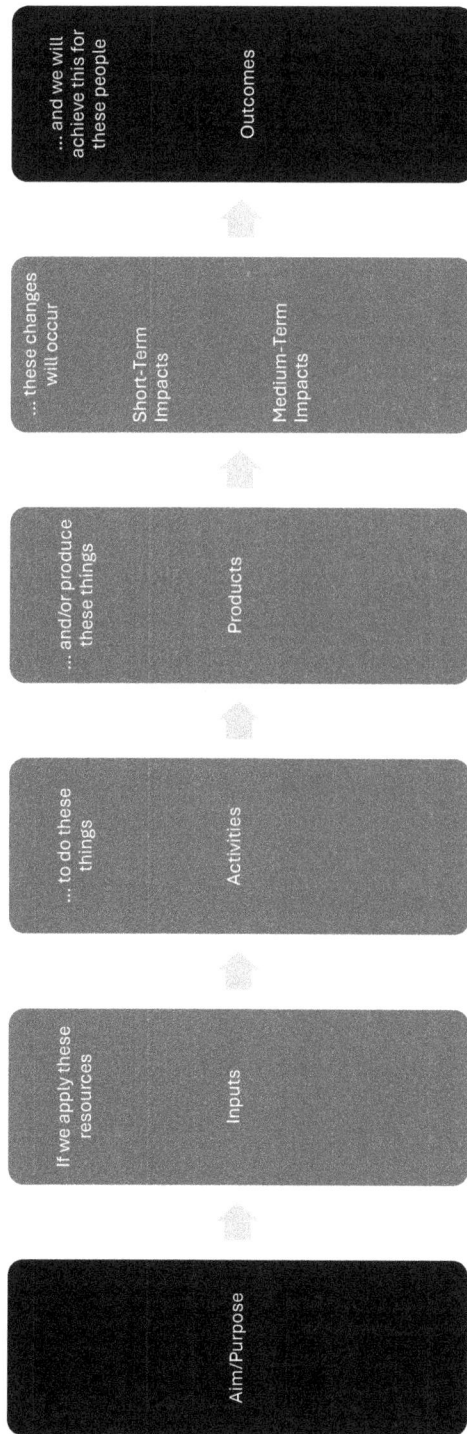

Figure 6.2 Logic Model Key Components

Ideally then, the first and last components of the logic model (aim and purpose / Impacts / Outcomes) are developed early in the policy development process so as to inform the development, implementation, and evaluation elements of the plan. Sometimes, that happens. Sometimes it doesn't.

Typically, policies are designed to support one or more existing organizational goals and indicators and targets for those goals have already been identified and are being reporting on. So at a high level, the monitoring and evaluation framework tends to be in place and well established before the policy development process even begins.

Also typically, there is more than one policy attached to any specific organizational goal (remember the network of policies we talked about in Chapter 2), and each of those policies will have a part to play, a specific and unique purpose in the overall strategy to achieve that goal. That drives the purpose of the individual policy and the results or lower-level goals it is intended to achieve. These lower level goals are sometimes not articulated in measurable terms, indicators and targets are not identified, and the ways of collecting and reporting on them are not put into place until a deeper dive or an evaluation is triggered. Where this happens, "monitoring" tends to focus on compliance alone, and, if and when evaluations are triggered, the process gets more complicated, longer, and more costly because there is no framework, logic model, or data available to inform it. The evaluator will need to retrace the thinking in the scoping exercise and develop the framework and logic model after the fact.

Regardless of when the framework and logic model are developed, their usefulness is dependent on the availability of data and a baseline against which progress can be measured.

Rise to the Challenge

Evaluation is essential. It is not easy. There are numerous challenges, including these:

- *Defining measurable objectives.* Many organizational policies, such as those relating to corporate culture or ethics, are inherently difficult to quantify. For example, if an organization has a policy aimed at fostering innovation, how can "innovation" be measured in a way that captures the policy's true impact?

- *Lack of clarity.* What is being assessed and how the assessment will be carried out are often ambiguous concepts, or they are clear in the mind of one person and clear—but very different— in the mind of someone else. There needs to be a solid and agreed-upon foundation for evaluation.
- *Objectivity and bias.* Three types of bias are potentially at play when you evaluate a policy.
  - *Implicit bias* occurs automatically and unintentionally because we are not aware of it. Nevertheless, it affects judgments, decisions, and behaviors.
  - *Confirmation bias* is the tendency to search for, interpret, favor, and recall information in a way that confirms or supports one's existing beliefs or values. Again, this may be unintentional, but it has unwanted impacts.
  - *Anchoring bias* is a cognitive bias that causes us to rely too heavily on the first piece of information we are given about a topic. We interpret newer information from the reference point of our anchor instead of seeing it objectively.

Bias in one form or another always exists, but it can be mitigated. Here are a few options to consider:

  - Agree on specific goals.
  - Ask relevant questions, in particular ones that challenge assumptions around issues like equity.
  - Develop a clear evaluation plan. A lack of guidelines for the evaluation process almost inevitably leads to bias.
  - Look at performance metrics.
  - Gather feedback from multiple sources.
  - Use an external evaluator.
- *Attribution and contribution.* Many factors can influence policy outcomes making it difficult to attribute changes directly to the policy itself. For instance, a policy aimed at increasing employee engagement might be affected by external economic conditions, leadership changes, or technological shifts. It's critical to, as objectively as possible, assess if the change you're seeing is due to the policy. It is also important to remember that the evaluation process itself can contribute to some of the changes you are seeing.

There are several things you can do to assess levels of attribution and contribution.

- *Conduct a counterfactual impact evaluation.* This is an assessment of what would have happened if the policy did not actively exist.
- *Examine the consistency of evidence.* Did the changes you're seeing evolve as expected or is there something unexpected?
- *Rule out other alternatives.* Take a deep and honest look at what else may have caused the changes you're seeing.

Policy Evaluation Data

Effective policy evaluation requires a structured and methodical approach to data collection and analysis.

Without this, there is no evaluation. You must have necessary and sufficient "data," in whatever form that takes, to answer evaluation questions in "measurable" terms with a "measurable" degree of confidence. Easy-peasy.

It helps to understand what data it is you need to collect. Three factors come into this understanding. First, the criteria you are using. These are the high-level standards that must be met. Quite simply, this is the way that success has been defined. The criteria can look different depending on the type of evaluation you are undertaking:

Developmental

- **Relevance**: Most likely (of the options) to achieve the intended objectives
- **Value:** Most likely to meet cost, opportunity cost, return-on-investment (ROI) targets
- **Time:** Most likely to meet implementation and ROI timelines

Outcome/Impact

- **Overall:** The degree to which policy objectives/targets have been met.
- **Effective/Impact:** The contribution of the policy to achieving those objectives and targets.

- **Equity:** The difference it made across all of the communities impacted.
- **Efficiency:** The use and cost of resources; how well are they are being used.
- **Sustainability:** Whether the benefits last.

Process

- **Completion:** The human and technical/infrastructure requirements have been fully addressed.
- **Compliance:** Everyone who needs to is complying with the policy.

Next in development of the data collection process is getting more specific about those criteria—making them measurable by identifying *indicators* that will provide insight into the criteria and determining the *targets* you want to attain—success. Knowing this will help to gather relevant and measurable data. It also scopes the data collection exercise: what data about what population over what period of time to answer what question.

Types of Evaluation Data

Policy evaluation is evaluation, and there are basics that help ensure any evaluation is effective. It starts with understanding the two main types of evaluation data that can be used—qualitative and quantitative.

Qualitative data focus on the experiential. Such data is often collected using methodologies such as on observation or interviews including focus groups, surveys with open-ended questions, and social media. Qualitative analyses tend to focus on the identification of themes that run through the data collected.

Quantitative data is numeric and measurable. Measurement-based tools, such as structured surveys and tracking programs, are used to generate the statistics and data which is then analyzed to identify trends, calculate key indicators such as variance and or probability and to make inferences to inform the evaluation.

How do you determine what approach, or approaches, your evaluation needs?

Consider these factors:

- Availability: How "available" are the data? What level of effort, time, and cost will be involved to access the data and/or implement the methodology?
- Completeness: How complete is the data set or range and statistical credibility of the views collected?
- Timeliness (Relevance): When were the data generated, what timeframe do they speak to, and is the timeframe relevant?
- Credibility: What is the source of the data? Is it a credible source?
- Impact on operation: Will staff be deferred or distracted to support the exercise and to what extent?

Bottom Line

Multiple ways of collecting data are generally preferred.

Ultimately, policy evaluation provides more than just a snapshot of what's working and what's not; it informs the policy planning and development process ensuring that organizations can know when and how to pivot and refine their approach in response to new challenges and opportunities. As organizations face increasing demands for transparency, efficiency, and sustainability, the role of robust policy evaluation will only become more important in shaping organizational outcomes and driving long-term success.

Bottom Line

Evaluation is essential.

About the Authors

Rose Landry

Rose has over 25 years' experience working on and leading policy initiatives; advising and coaching leaders; and mentoring and training professionals at every level of the not-for-profit, private, and public sectors.

She is the owner of Landry & Associates Management Consulting, a boutique firm that has been providing consulting and advisory services to clients across Canada for over 20 years.

In addition to her work as a consultant, Rose has served as a senior executive in both the public and private sectors and as a Board Member with multiple not-for-profit organizations. She has been involved in education and training throughout her career—designing and managing individualized training programs for the World University Service of Canada, authoring and delivering Dalhousie University/Henson College's course on Organizational Structure & Design and serving as a guest lecturer for their MBA and MPA programs; and Co- developing and delivering the Policy Certificate program at Saint Mary's University's Executive and Professional Development Program with donalee Moulton.

donalee Moulton

donalee Moulton has more than 25 years' experience in communications. She is the owner of Quantum Communications, a communications company based in Halifax. As a consultant, donalee has provided clients across Canada, the United States, and beyond with a wide range of services, including comprehensive policy writing, communications, and review, and editorial services, media relations, government relations, and communications planning. Her clients include the World Health Organization, Justice Canada, the Canadian International Development Agency, the Canadian MedicAlert Foundation, Deloitte & Touche, and Pfizer Inc.

In addition to her communications work, donalee is a professional journalist. Her byline has appeared in more than 100 magazines and newspapers throughout North America, including *The National Post*, *Investment Executive*, *The Lawyers Weekly*, *The Medical Post*, *Equinox*, *Chatelaine*, *The Globe & Mail*, and *The Bottom Line*. donalee is the author of *The Thong Principle: Saying What You Mean and Meaning What You Say*, published by Business Expert Press.

donalee co-developed the Policy Certificate program for Saint Mary's University's Executive and Professional Development program with Rose Landry, and she has taught policy writing and communicating policy for organizations across North America. donalee has also taught business communication for the past 20 years in a variety of programs, including the Bachelor of Commerce Program at Dalhousie University and both the Certificate for Management and the Management Diploma Programs at Saint Mary's University. She also taught in Mount Saint Vincent University's Public Relations Degree program.

Index

www.ingramcontent.com/pod-product-compliance
Lightning Source LLC
Chambersburg PA
CBHW061326220326
41599CB00026B/5053